D0365485

THE POEMS OF GEORGE CRABBE

THE REV. GEORGE CRABBE, LL.B., J.P.

(After the painting by T. Phillips, R.A.   In the possession of John Murray, Esq.)

"*The Poems of George Crabbe*"   Frontispiece.

THE POEMS OF
GEORGE CRABBE

A LITERARY & HISTORICAL STUDY

By the Rev.

J. H. EVANS, B.A., Hon.C.F.

(British Archæological Associate)
Vicar of Croxton Kerrial, and Rector of Branston-by-Belvoir
Leicestershire

As imagination bodies forth
The forms of things unknown, the poet's pen
Turns them to shapes, and gives to airy nothing
A local habitation and a name.

Shakespeare.

LONDON
THE SHELDON PRESS
NORTHUMBERLAND AVENUE, W.C. 2
NEW YORK: THE MACMILLAN CO.

First Published - - - - 1933

Printed in Great Britain

THIS BOOK

SO INTIMATELY CONNECTED WITH

LORDLY BELVOIR

IS DEDICATED BY PERMISSION TO

HIS GRACE

THE DUKE OF RUTLAND

THE POET'S PREFACE TO "TALES"

THE poet is one who, in the excursions of his fancy between heaven and earth, lights upon a fairy-land in which he places a creation of his own, where he embodies shapes, and gives action and adventure to his ideal offspring. Taking captive the imagination of his readers, he elevates them above the grossness of actual being into the soothing and pleasant atmosphere of supra-mundane existence. There he obtains for his visionary inhabitants attentive interest and moderate sympathy which the realities of nature oftentimes fail to produce, either because they are so familiar and insignificant that they excite no determinate emotion, or are so harsh and powerful that the feelings excited are grating and distasteful. . . .

All satire wherein character is skilfully delineated must no longer be esteemed as genuine poetry, and for the same reason many affecting narratives which are founded on real events, and borrow no aid whatever from the imagination of the writer, must likewise be rejected. A considerable part of the poems of Chaucer are of this naked and unveiled character, and there are in his "Tales" many pages of coarse, accurate, and minute, but very striking description. Many small poems in a subsequent age, of most impressive kind, are adapted and addressed to the common sense of the reader, and prevail by the strong language of truth and nature. . . .

Dryden has given us much of this poetry, in which the force of expression and accuracy of description have neither needed nor obtained assistance from the fancy of the writer. Pope himself has no small portion of this actuality of relation, this nudity of description and poetry without an atmosphere; the lines beginning " In the worst inn's worst room" are an example, and many others may be seen in his Satires. The frequent absence of those " Sports of Fancy" and " Tricks of Strong Imagination" have been so much observed, that some have ventured to question whether even this writer were a poet; and though, as Dr. Johnson has remarked, it would be difficult to form a definition in which Pope should not be admitted. . . .

Having thus far presumed to claim for the ensuing pages the rank and title of poetry, I attempt no more, nor venture to class or compare them with any other kinds of poetical composition; their place will doubtless be found for them.

A principal view and wish of the poet must be to engage the mind of his readers, as failing in that point, he will scarcely succeed in any other: I therefore willingly confess that much of my time and assiduity has been devoted to this purpose; but, to the ambition of pleasing, no other sacrifices have, I trust, been made, than of my own labour and care. Nothing will be found that militates against the rules of propriety and good manners, nothing that offends against the more important precepts of morality and religion; and with this negative kind of merit, I commit my book to the judgment and taste of the reader—not being willing to provoke his vigilance by professions of accuracy, nor to solicit his indulgence by apologies for mistakes.

GEORGE CRABBE.

Muston,
   July 31, 1812.

FOREWORD

BELVOIR CASTLE,
GRANTHAM.
August 13th, 1932.

DEAR MR. EVANS,

Thank you for so kindly letting me have an opportunity to read the MS. of such an interesting history as that of the great poet Crabbe.

As a result of your investigations, many verses in the chapters dealing with my family and this neighbourhood cast fresh light upon the life and manners of the eighteenth century, and I have much pleasure in recommending it to the public.

Yours sincerely,

RUTLAND.

AUTHOR'S NOTE

THE following chapters have been selected, revised, and expanded out of certain historical essays and other literary articles on " The Poet Crabbe," lately contributed to *The Grantham Journal*. They attempt to describe the main features, associations, traditions, and legends concerning that writer and his poems after the somewhat novel style first suggested by Edward FitzGerald's readings or annotations.

Their chief substance is based upon reliable resources like his son's biography, county and local histories, parochial records and family manuscripts referred to now and again in the text. The casual discovery, from rarely known facts, that the author of " The Parish Register " occasionally resided at Croxton Kerrial Park House during the ducal chaplaincy, and later on held the incumbency in plurality for nearly twenty years, led to a study of his various compositions. It was then seen quite plainly that a large section dealt with material more or less maritime, naturally affecting the Suffolk homes and East Coast generally. But, on the other hand, smaller portions, such as belonged an inland estate, often contained suggestive topographical incidents better adapted to centre round the Belvoir Country habitations particularly; and therefore those verses have received rather fuller consideration.

This being the centenary year of the poet's death, the work has been prepared for publication in book form by request, and with the hope that it may be found much more interesting than in the previous serial issue.

J. H. E.

September 30, 1932.

CONTENTS

APPENDICES

CHRONOLOGICAL ORDER OF CHIEF COMPOSITIONS REFERRED TO IN CONTENTS

LIST OF ILLUSTRATIONS

CHAPTER I

CRABBE'S BIRTH, HOME AND SCHOOL LIFE

O happy child ! the glorious day shall shine,
When every ear shall to thy speech incline,
Thy words alluring and thy voice divine:
The sullen pedant and the sprightly wit,
To hear thy soothing eloquence shall sit;
And both, abjuring Flattery, will agree
That truth inspires, and they must honour thee.[1]

GEORGE CRABBE was born on Christmas-eve, 1754, at Aldeburgh, Suffolk, where the family name is still fairly common in this or the shorter form of spelling. The poet himself humorously said: " I cannot account for the vanity of that one of my ancestors who first (dissatisfied with the four letters which composed the name Crab, the sour fruit, or Crab, the crusty fish) added his *be* by way of disguise. Alas ! he gained nothing worth his trouble, but he has brought on me, his descendant, after I know not how many generations, a question beyond my abilities to answer." All efforts to trace an established descent were unsuccessful according to his son, who proceeds to say: " Various branches of the name appear to have been settled from a remote period in Norfolk, and in different sea-faring places on the coast of Suffolk, and it seems probable that the first who assumed it was a fisherman. A pilot, by name Crabbe, of Walton, was consulted as a man of remarkable experience about the voyage of Edward the Third, previous to the Battle of Cressy. The Crabbes of Norfolk have been for many generations in the station of farmers or wealthy yeomen, and I doubt whether any of the race had ever risen much above this sphere of life, for, though there is now in the possession

[1] " The Birth of Flattery."

of my uncle at Southwold an apparently ancient coat of arms, how or whence it came into the hands of his father we have no trace, and, therefore, I cannot attach much weight to such a shadowy token of ' gentle ' pretensions." The grandfather, a collector of customs, held an important minor position in the borough of the Alde. For this little town, from the sixteenth-century onwards, possessed some consequential rights, under ancient Royal charters, such as the privilege of returning two Members to Parliament. Its chief magistrates were bailiffs, Justices of the Peace, who presided over the Court of Sessions with ten capital and twenty-four burgesses. Mr. Crabbe belonged to the latter, and owing to his connection with Trinity House, would be respected by the common fishing folk much in the same way as the lower look upon the middle classes today. Therefore he not unnaturally desired to give his son as good an education as possible; and so we find George's father, up to a few years before the poet's birth, having charge of Norton Village School, in Norfolk; then, later on, settled at his native place as Saltmaster. And it is stated that his early training had made him a distinguished mathematician, and rather fond of English literature. Here he married a young widow with the most amiable disposition: mild, patient, affectionate, and deeply religious. Their first child, George, the eldest of four brothers, was brought up in an old range of buildings along the crooked mole which served as a harbour for the shipping. Stanfield, the artist, in Crabbe's Poetical Works,[1] gives us a good view of Aldeburgh, less than a mile south-east from the present beach near Slaughden, which owing to sea encroachments and violent storms disappeared long ago. All we know about the houses is that they were, in general, mean and ill-constructed. One, apparently, belonged to the family for two or three generations. It had a thatched roof and gables.

[1] *The Poetical Works of the Rev. George Crabbe*, 1834. 8 vols. (John Murray.)

Some upper parts projected over the main floor. The windows were small, filled with diamond-leaded panes almost impervious to the light. Now, owing to its position, Crabbe's parents used it not only for official, but also for store purposes, after they purchased the half-share in a " hoy "—vessels employed in the trade of the port.

> Yon is our quay. Those smaller hoys from town
> Its various ware, for country use, bring down;
> Those laden waggons, in return, impart
> The country produce to the city mart.
> Hark to the clamour in that miry road,
> Bounded and narrow'd by yon vessel's load;
> The lumbering wealth she empties round the place,
> Package and parcel, hogshead, chest, and case,
> While the loud seamen and the angry hind,
> Mingling in business, bellow to the wind.

From this noisy, busy, uncongenial spot, the young poet first saw the light, the sea, the shore, and its ill-bred, churlish folk, " with sullen woe display'd in every face "; but showed no great desire to seek a nautical career, and so his father felt concerned for his future. " That boy," he would say, " must be a fool. John and Bob and Will are all of some use about a boat, but what will that thing ever be good for ?" He, however, soon discovered his liking for poetry, through the nightly practice of reading aloud to the little ones certain authors who had pleased him when a school-master. Years after, the son recalls these early associations with the muse:

> When the long dull day
> Has slowly passed in weary tasks away,
> To other worlds with cheerful view he looks
> And parts the night between repose and books.
> Amid his labours he has sometimes tried
> To turn a little from his cares aside—
> Pope, Milton, Dryden, with delight has seized,
> His soul engaged, and of his trouble eased.[1]

[1] " The Borough."

Still, we have little reason, if any, for supposing
that because the boy did not desire to be a sailor,
like at least two of his brothers, he had no fondness
for the sea. John is known to have served for some
time in the Royal Navy, was subsequently promoted
captain to a Liverpool slave-ship, and ended his life
most tragically through its mutinous crew.   William—

> A strong and handsome stripling he became,
> And the gay spirit answer'd to the frame;
> A lighter, happier lad was never seen,
> For ever easy, cheerful, or serene—

followed suit, and his adventures among the Spaniards
afforded material for one of the poet's most thrilling
tales illustrated by Allan Booth in " The Parting Hour."
On the contrary, there are many indications both in
his life and works showing how much he loved the
water. For example, his father bought a small sailing
boat in order to navigate the river Alde. Now the
first event deeply impressed upon the child's mind
seems to have been a voyage in this frail vessel. It
happened thus. Some few amateur yachtsmen belonging to the town club were anxious to try the new
purchase, and his fond mother obtained permission
for George to be one of the company. He has recorded
the experience in the following lines:

> Sweet was the morning's breath, the inland tide,
> And our boat gliding where alone could glide
> Small craft—and they oft touch'd on either side.
> It was my first-born joy—I heard them say
> " Let the child go: he will enjoy the day,
> For children ever feel delighted when
> They take their portion and enjoy with men."

Besides what he has himself told us, it is almost
impossible to imagine one like him not wanting to
join his little brothers in their games with others
when:

ALDEBURGH—"THE BOROUGH
Drawn by C. Stanfield, A.R.A.

THE HOUSE OF CRABBE'S FATHER.
Drawn by C. Stanfield, A.R.A.

facing p. 4.

Dabbling on shore half-naked sea-boys crowd,
Swim round a ship, or swing upon the shroud;
Or in a boat purloin'd, with paddles play,
And grow familiar with the watery way:
Young though they be they feel whose sons they are,
They know what British seamen do and dare;
Proud of that fame, they raise and they enjoy
The rustic wonder of the village boy.

Having been cradled among the sons of " a wild,
amphibious race," we find him in infancy and frequently in after-life:

Attentive, listening, in the moving scene,
And often wondering what the men could mean,
When ships at sea made signals of their need,
I watched on shore the sailors and their speed,
Mixed in their act, nor rested till I knew
Why they were call'd, and what they had to do.
Whatever business in the past was done,
I without call, was with the busy one:
Not daring question but with open ear
And greedy spirit ever bent to hear.
To me the wives of seamen loved to tell
What storms endanger'd men esteem'd so well;
What wond'rous things in foreign parts they saw,
Lands without bounds, and people without law.
No ships were wreck'd upon that fatal beach,
But I could give the luckless tale of each;
Eager I look'd, till I beheld a face
Of one disposed to paint their dismal case;
Who gave the sad survivors' doleful tale,
From the first brushing of the mighty gale
Until they struck; and, suffering in their fate,
I long'd the more they should its horrors state;
While some, the fond of pity, would enjoy
The earnest sorrows of the feeling boy.
There were fond girls, who took me to their side
To tell the story how their lovers died;[1]
In fact, I lived for many an idle year
In fond pursuit of agitations dear;

[1] See Appendix II.

> For ever seeking, ever pleased to find,
> The food I loved, I thought not of its kind;
> It gave affliction while it brought delight,
> And joy and anguish could at once excite.

The ex-schoolmaster obviously appreciated sound mental training, and no doubt desired to further the interests of his boys, but being employed now daily in commerce and the customs would be quite unable to instruct them personally. His mother, though well versed in Holy Scripture, but wearied with constant cares for her little family, could hardly be expected to do so, save on Sundays. They, however, were not without helpful resources at Aldeburgh. As the poet says:

> To every class we have a School assign'd,
> Rules for all ranks, and food for every mind,
>
> .   .   .   .
>
> Poor Reuben Dixon has the noisiest School
> Of ragged lads who ever bow'd to rule.
> Low in his price, the men who heave our coals
> And clean our causeways send him boys in shoals.

Reference is also made to another person, this one a lady—

> Of superior kind,
> For higher Schools prepares the rising mind;
> Preparatory she her learning calls—
> The step first made to Colleges and Halls.

But to neither establishment did the Crabbes send their little children, for he adds:

> Yet one there is that small regard to rule
> Or study pays, and still is deem'd a School;
> That where a deaf, poor, patient widow sits,
> And awes some thirty infants as she knits—
> Infants of humble, busy wives, who pay
> Some trifling price for freedom through the day.
> At this good matron's hut the children meet,
> Who thus becomes the mother of the street.

This picture with youngsters at play after school, must have been printed upon his mind at the time with others, as given elsewhere:

> None heed the stagnant pools on either side
> Where new launch'd ships of infant sailors ride.
> Rodneys in rags here British valour boast,
> And lisping Nelsons fright the Gallic coast;
> They fix the rudder, set the swelling sail,
> They point the bowsprit and they blow the gale.
> True to her port the frigate sails away,
> And o'er that frowning ocean finds her bay;
> Her owner rigg'd her, and he knows her worth
> And sees her, fearless, gunwhale deep go forth.
> Dreadless he views his sea by breezes curl'd
> When inch-high billows vex the watery world.

During these early days the young poet used to write verses somewhat like those read aloud by his father, and eventually many of them were published in a monthly magazine. Now for an unknown reason he did not continue at school here, and consequently it has been disputed whether any free education could be had at that time. If so, we cannot understand the parents not wanting to profit by the privilege.

We know they were somewhat concerned about the child's precocity. Possibly the " mother of the street," elated by her little scholar's attainments, somewhat overtaxed his brain, judging from the lines in the " Tale of the Learned Boy ":

> Meanwhile the Dame was anxious day and night,
> To guide the notions of her babe aright,
> And on the favourite mind to throw her glimmering light;
> Her Bible stories she impressed betimes,
> And fill'd his head with hymns and holy rhymes,
> On powers unseen the good and ill she dwelt,
> And the poor boy mysterious terrors felt.

Anyhow, they resolved to send George to Bungay where he spent four years with little to recall except that he nearly lost his life in this way. He and several other schoolfellows were punished for playing at soldiers by being put into a large dog-kennel, known by the terrible name of "The Black Hole." George first entered, and the place being crammed full with offenders, the atmosphere soon became pestilentially close. The poor boy in vain shrieked that he was about to be suffocated. At last, in despair, he bit the lad next to him violently in the hand. "Crabbe is dying! Crabbe is dying!" roared the sufferer, and the sentinel at length opened the door and allowed the boys to rush out into the air. "A minute more and I must have died," he told his son. Afterwards, in the year 1765, he went to an important school at Stowmarket, situated in the centre of the county, and kept by Mr. Richard Haddon, a skilful mathematician, under whom he spent the next three years, with an annual holiday in the summer, but each time returning very reluctantly, for it seems that the bigger boys treated him badly, especially one:

> The Tyrant boy, whose sway
> All hearts acknowledged; him the crowds obey.
> At his command they break through every rule.
> Whoever governs, he controls the School.

However, the biographer informs us that, "inheriting his father's talent and predilection for science, he made considerable progress in such pursuits and undoubtedly in his favourite poetical studies." But he himself has little, if anything, to say beyond:

> Of all the good that grew of early date,
> I can but parts and incidents relate:
> A guest arriving, or a borrow'd day
> From school, or schoolboy triumph at some play:
> And these from Pain may be deduced; for these
> Removed some ill, and hence their power to please.

CHAPTER II

And thou too, Boy ! wilt pass unheeding by,
The scenes that now delight thine eager eye.
Dream on awhile ! and there shall come a strange
And could'st thou see it, an amazing change.
. . . for in that place a room
Should be thine own, thy house, thy hall, thy home,
With leave to wander as thou wouldst to read
Just as thy fancy was disposed to feed.[1]

WHEN it was decided that George should become a doctor, he left Stowmarket in his fourteenth year. But those were apprenticeship days, and some months elapsed before anyone would undertake the training. However, towards the close of 1768 an opening was found with a country practitioner and agriculturist, at Wickhambrook, not so far from Cheveley Park, the Newmarket seat of the Duke of Rutland, where soon he used to deliver his master's medicine. Here—

The lad one morning—it was his custom now—
Walk'd and conversed with labourers at the plough,
With threshers hastening to their daily task,
With woodmen resting o'er the enlivening flask,
And with the shepherd, watchful of his fold
Beneath the hill, and pacing in the cold;
Further afield he sometimes would proceed,
And take a path wherever it might lead.
    It led him far about to Wickham Green,
Where stood the mansion of the village queen;
Her garden yet its wintry blossoms bore,
And roses graced the windows and the door—

[1] " Silford Hall."

9

That lasting kind, that through the varying year
Or in the bud or in the bloom appear;
All flowers that now the gloomy days adorn
Rose on the view, and smiled upon that morn.

Before half the statutory seven years were spent in what
proved to be more the farmhouse than the dispensary,
his parents transferred him to a town surgeon at
Woodbridge, named Page, whose medical connection
must have been considerable, seeing that reference is
made in the *Works* to an assistant, Dr. Goodwin, the
learned author on physics:

And some by learning—young physicians write,
To set their merit in the fairest light.

Having an excellent memory, he had committed
practically all Shakespeare to heart, together with
much gossip and many tales heard when acting as
errand boy. At the former place he filled a large
drawer with verses, and in the latter composed a poem
on " Hope," which gained a prize, with four others,
signed " G. C. Woodbridge, Suffolk, 1772." But the
most remarkable production was a lengthy satire
called " Inebriety," based upon Pope's style, beginning thus:

The mighty spirit, and its power which stains . . .
The gentle fair on nervous tea relies,
Whilst gay good nature sparkles in her eyes;
Champagne the courtier drinks, the spleen to chase,
The Colonel burgundy, and port His Grace.

There are nearly two hundred additional couplets
more or less connected, originally issued in pamphlet
form at Ipswich. The juvenile author now began
coming into contact with other young men of social
and intellectual equality, for we find his companions
were members of a Literary Club, held weekly at an
inn. These circumstances undoubtedly contributed to
the above composition, for which Crabbe in later life

felt heartily ashamed. It even looks as though he
were so at the time.

> Applause from hands the dying accents break,
> Of staggering sots who vainly try to speak;
> At weekly Club to flourish, where he rules,
> The glorious president of grosser fools.
>
> .   .   .
>
> Enough of these, and all the charms of wine,
> Be sober joys and social evenings mine.

During the apprenticeship at Woodbridge, a distressing change happened at home. Mr. Crabbe,
always deeply engrossed in politics, had lately become
local agent for the Whig candidate, and unfortunately
gave way to drinking bouts which greatly distressed
the family. Then, because of his behaviour, he was
no longer allowed to act as Churchwarden, lost
much town shipping connection, and in consequence
became a poorer man. George, therefore, on return,
instead of proceeding " to the Metropolis to complete
his professional education," had to stay at Aldeburgh,
assist the parents, and take any appointment for which
he was already qualified. It seemed the burgesses
were anxious to recognise and encourage him from the
outset, for the Board of Guardians records in its minute
book dated September 17th, 1775, " that Mr. George
Crabbe shall be employed to cure the boy Howard of
the itch, and that whenever any of the poor shall have
occasion for a surgeon the overseers shall apply to him
for that purpose." Thus we observe him visiting the
Parish Workhouse.

> But soon a loud and hasty summons calls,
> Shakes the thin roof, and echoes round the walls;
> Anon, a figure enters quaintly neat,
> All pride and business, bustle and conceit;
> With looks unalter'd by these scenes of woe.
> With speed that entering, speaks his haste to go,
> He bids the gazing throng around him fly,
> And carries fate and physic in his eye.

The young man, however, felt dissatisfied with this engagement, especially from the surgical point of view. So he persuaded his father to send him to a new hospital, endowed by Mr. Guy, the rich bookseller, and now known after his name.

> Hence yonder Building rose: on either side
> Far stretch'd the wards, all airy, warm, and wide;
> And every ward has beds by comfort spread,
> And smooth'd for him who suffers on the bed.
> How rose the Building ?   Piety first laid
> A strong foundation, but she wanted aid;
> To Wealth, unwieldy was her prayer address'd,
> Who largely gave, and she the donor bless'd.

Here, then, for the present the inmates could see him—

> Observing every ward as round he goes,
> He thinks what pain, what danger they enclose;
> Fevers and chronic ills, corroding pains,
> Each accidental mischief man sustains:
> Fractures and wounds, and wither'd limbs and lame,
> With all that, slow or sudden, vex our frame.

But after a few months the lectures in connection with the medical course, during Crabbe's first visit to London, were cut short for want of means. Consequently he returned home, in little less than a year, with disappointing prospects. Still, this untoward event ultimately made him one of England's foremost poets, because, apart from the abrupt ending to his training, he lacked sufficient confidence in himself, and therefore did not take kindly to the profession. So, after acting as assistant to Mr. Maskill, an apothecary at Aldeburgh, he came into his master's failing business through a free gift. But he could have little hope to succeed. Indeed, it seems Crabbe had made botany a special hobby; and " even this very passion was injurious; for ignorant patients seeing him return from his walks, with handfuls of weeds, decided that

as the Doctor got his medicines in the ditches, he could
have little claim for payment !" Again, there were
many poor relations, who daily " requested something
comfortable from cousin George "—that is to say,
doses of the most expensive tonics in his possession.
Then, lastly, " the sense of a new responsibility
pressed sorely and continually on his mind, so that
he never awoke without shuddering at the thought
that a difficult operation might be thrown in his way
before night." One or two cases in the *Works* illustrate this sentiment. For example, when explaining
the conduct of the infidel poacher in the " Parish
Register "—

> Each village inn has heard the ruffian boast
> That he believed in " neither God nor ghost "—

he is referring to the village blacksmith, at Leiston,
near Aldeburgh, whose hardened character made a
strong impression upon the surgeon when amputating
the man's hand in 1779. Said he: " I suppose, Doctor
Crabbe, I shall get it again at the resurrection !" We
have the dreadful sequel, with his own guarded conclusion, thus expressed:

> What age and sickness for a man so bold
> Had done, we know not—none beheld him old.
> By night, as business urged, he sought the wood;
> The ditch was deep—the rain had caused a flood,
> The foot-bridge fail'd—he plunged beneath the deep,
> And slept, if truth were his, th' eternal sleep.

About this time a Woodbridge medical friend,
William Springall Levett, son of an Aldeburgh surgeon,
introduced him to the person who more than anybody
else helped to shape his future career. William said
carelessly one day, " Why, George, you shall go with
me to Parham; there is a young lady there that would
just suit you." This meeting decided his matrimonial
lot in life. Levett, however, died shortly after, much

to the regret of all who knew him, and the budding
poet then composed the following striking epitaph:

> What ! though no trophies peer above his dust,
> Nor sculptured conquests deck his sober bust;
> What ! though no earthly thunders sound his name,
> Death gives him conquest and our sorrows fame;
> One sigh reflection heaves, but shuns excess—
> More should we mourn him, did we love him less.[1]

Sarah Elmy was born and baptised the same day,
December 12th, 1751, at Beccles. Her parents had
recently possessed a tanning factory, but the father,
having failed in business, went to Guadeloupe, where he
died (some time before Mr. Crabbe knew the family).
The widow, it seems, remained in the town, just
managing to exist, with a small family, on the yearly
income of £100, part being derived from her own
right—the interest upon £1,500 capital—the other
made up by her brother, a wealthy gentleman farmer,
John Tovell, Esq., Parham Hall, Suffolk, who also
contributed towards the educational expenses of the
children and their general welfare. Here the eldest
daughter made periodical long stays, during one of
which the engagement took place, presumably in the
garden; for years after we are told:

> Oh ! days remember'd well ! remember'd all !
> The bitter sweet, the honey, and the gall;
> Those garden rambles in the silent night,
> Those trees so shady, and that moon so bright;
> That thick-set alley by the arbor closed,
> That woodbine seat, where we at last reposed;
> And then the hopes that came and then were gone . . .
> Now in this instant shall my love be shown.

The day itself is not recorded. It must, however,
have been a red-letter one in the poet's early life. Now
for the first time, young Crabbe, like his imaginary

---

[1] 1774, Green's *History of Framlingham*.

knights, had his own heroine, the lady to whom he gave the pretty name Mira (or Myra), which is supposed to be an abbreviated combination of the last two syllables in Elmy, Sarah. Thus, at last, from the fairest of the fair sex, his gifted talent met with the highest appreciation and encouragement, resulting in the publication of many lyrics in a lady's magazine, which eventually brought him distinction, as the following lines in a prize poem indicate:

> But, above all, the poet owns thy powers—
> Hope leads him on, and every fear devours;
> He writes, and unsuccessful, writes again,
> Nor thinks the last laborious work in vain;
> New schemes he forms and various plots he tries,
> To win the laurel, and possess the prize.[1]

Miss Elmy rendered many useful and kindly services during a lengthy engagement, not only in encouraging the composition of verses, but also in directing the course of the poet's career. Indeed, but for her discretion and solid support at this very critical period the young doctor, with insufficient credentials, would have settled down precariously in a profession for which he had little taste and less nerve. It is true, as the son informs us, in affectionate remembrance, " that the chief consolation of all his father's distresses at this period was the knowledge that he had gained a faithful and affectionate heart at Parham. ' My Mira came ! be ever blest the hour.' " Still, neither the one nor the other has afforded enough particulars to picture clearly in our minds this charming little lady. Every descriptive feature and quality published in the earliest poems has disappeared. All we know for certain is that she possessed a " remarkably pretty " appearance, so like a child's beautiful face, full of innocence. Morally, she was said to have been " lively and cheerful "; very prudent and resolute; endowed

[1] *Wheble's Magazine*, 1772.

by nature with " great penetration and acuteness, a
firm, unflinching spirit, and a warm and feeling heart."
One of her letters verifies this latter statement, and also
confirms the fact that the poet sought and acted upon
Myra's advice, even in choosing a publisher for one
of his earliest and best known works. She writes: " I
am obliged to you, my dearest Mr. Crabbe, for taking
my opinion respecting Mr. Dodsley. If you had none
of your own, the compliment would not be very great,
but as you are much better calculated to instruct than
to be instructed, I must be always proud to give my
opinion, and pleased to see it adopted. It is said, you
know, we learn anything better from those we love."[1]
Many indirect references are easily found in several
poems. For example, when portraying the characters
of " The Sisters," the author obviously had Myra in
mind for Lucy, whose smile

> . . . . approval told,
> Cheerful, not changing neither kind nor cold.
> Lucy loved all that grew upon the ground,
> And loveliness in all things living found;
> The gilded fly, the fern upon the wall,
> Were nature's works, and admirable all.

Then later in " The Mother ":

> There was such goodness, such pure nature seen
> In Lucy's looks, a manner so serene
> Such harmony, in motion, speech, and air,
> That wonderful fairness, she was more than fair,
> Had more than beauty in each speaking grace,
> That lent their cloudless glory to the face;
> Where mild good sense in placid looks was shown,
> And felt in every bosom but her own.

Or again, when the Norfolk Militia were quartered at
Aldeburgh in 1778 and he supposed one of the young
men, a kinsman in reality, to be making love to
Myra:

[1] Normanston, referring to " The Village."

With self-approval in his laughing face
His seem'd the leading spirit of the place;
She was all coldness—yet I thought a look,
But that corrected, tender welcome spoke.

.   .   ˙.   .

O ! how it grieved me that she dared t' excite
Those looks in him that show'd so much delight;
Egregious coxcomb ! there he smiled again
As if he sought to aggravate my pain.[1]

[1] " Tales of the Hall."

CHAPTER III

> Who, but the race, by Fancy's demon led,
> Starve by the means they use to gain their bread?
> Oft have I read, and, reading, mourn'd the fate
> Of garret-bard, and his unpitied mate;
> One trial past, let sober Reason speak;
> Here shall we rest, or shall we further seek?

EXISTENCE being practically impossible, the young doctor decided to abandon his medical profession, but not without a struggle to find whether he could overcome existing difficulties or not, so at the end of three years he writes:

> Time in my pathway strews few flowers
> To cheer or cheat the weary hours,
> And those few strangers, dear indeed,
> Are choked, are checked by many a weed.[1]

As the biographer says, " Conscious of possessing no ordinary abilities, he brooded with deep mortification on his failure." Still, notwithstanding this uncertainty, love for Myra fostered inspiration and consolation.

> Fame shall be mine. Then wealth shall I possess,
> And beauty next an ardent lover bless;
> For me the maid shall leave her nobler state,
> Happy to raise and share her poet's fate.[2]

It would appear that henceforth, owing to an illness, Miss Elmy began to influence her dear Mr. Crabbe

[1] " My Birthday," 1778. [2] " The Patron."

18

in a religious direction, judging from his solemn meditations: " The year of sorrow and care, of poverty and disgrace, of disappointment and wrong, is passing on to join the eternal. Now, O Lord, let I beseech Thee, my afflictions and prayers be remembered, let my faults and follies be forgotten."[1] In the spring of the following year, having no money, Crabbe borrowed £5 from Mr. Dudley North. Then, gathering several poems from their hiding-place, a few valuable surgical instruments (with a view to sale), and some personal belongings, he left the Slaughden quay on board a sloop, " to seek his fortune in the great city." This ship had three masts, not one, and happened to be the *Unity* lugger of Aldeburgh, owned by a wealthy old sea captain, Robinson Groome, grandfather of the noted Archdeacon of Suffolk whose grandson is today the well-known agent for the Belvoir Estate.[2] Having arrived in the Metropolis, our literary adventurer met with the common experience of other poverty-stricken eighteenth-century geniuses, like Goldsmith. For reference is made to his " loft " in Cornhill—the usual Grub-street garret. There he kept a " journal," and jotted down such touching, and often humorous, remarks as—" I don't think there's a man in London worth but fourpence-halfpenny—for I've this moment sent seven farthings for a pint of porter—who is so resigned to his poverty."[3] At last, when almost in despair, a benefactor appeared upon the scene— namely, Edmund Burke—who immediately altered the situation and made the poet. At all events, there is now, owing to this fortunate coincidence, no with-holding the " force of his genius." Amongst the verses submitted, justifying admiration and support, were these lines, so reminiscent of his departure from Aldeburgh:

[1] December 31st, 1779.
[2] *Two Suffolk Friends*, by F. H. Groome.
[3] May 10th.

As on the neighbouring beach yon swallows stand,
And wait for favouring winds to leave the land,
While still for flight the ready wing is spread,
So waited I the favourite hour—and fled;
Fled from these shores, where guilt and rapine reign,
And cried, " Ah ! hapless they who still remain—
Who still remain to hear the ocean roar,
Whose greedy waves devour the lessening shore."[1]

Again, looking back, Burke seems to say in " Tales of
the Hall ":

Years past away, and where he lived, and how,
Was then unknown—indeed we know not now;
But once at twilight walking up and down,
In a poor alley of the mighty town,
Where in her narrow courts and garrets hide
The grieving sons of genius, want, and pride,
I met him musing: sadness I could trace,
And conquer'd hope's meek anguish, in his face.

There are few incidents more touching and romantic
in Crabbe's life than his connection with this learned
and illustrious statesman, author of *The Sublime and
Beautiful*. Burke was a great reader and a devout son
of the Church. He loved country life and books, and
invited Crabbe to stay with him at Beaconsfield, to
improve his studies, for he had now decided upon his
future profession. We can almost see them as they
advance towards the well-lighted apartment, and hear
these words:

Come, child of care ! to make thy soul serene,
Approach the treasures of this tranquil scene;
Survey the dome, and as the doors unfold,
The soul's best cure, in all her cares, behold ![2]

Here, in congenial atmosphere, this poem, a work of
considerable length, was first published anonymously ;
but after the author had been introduced to several

---

[1] " The Village."   [2] " The Library."

such distinguished persons as Sir Joshua Reynolds, Dr. Samuel Johnson, and Lord Thurlow, three leading men in art, literature, and politics, the name soon leaked out. Indeed, the last, in order to make amends for not recognising genius sooner, invited the poet round to breakfast one morning, and said: " The first poem you sent me, sir, I ought to have noticed. . . . Accept this trifle in the meantime and rely on my embracing an early opportunity to serve you more substantially when I hear you are in Orders." The " trifling " amount turned out to be a handsome gift for £100 ! Long afterwards his son writes: " I am enabled to state—though the information never came from my father—that the first use he made of this good fortune was to seek out and relieve some objects of real indigence, poor scholars like himself, whom he had known when sharing their wretchedness in the city; and I must add, that whenever he visited London in later years, he made it his business to enquire after similar objects of charity, supposed to be of respectable personal character, and to do by them as, in his own hour of distress, he would have been done by." Many older parsons today can recall a favourite textbook of theirs not unknown to Crabbe, Butler's *Analogy of Religion*. With what joy, then, did he apply himself to master this and kindred works in order to further satisfy the Lord Chancellor, who made no mistake and meant what he said, having only recently read:

> To thee, Divinity ! to thee, the light
> And guide of mortals, through their mental night;
> By whom we learn our hopes and fears to guide.
> To bear with pain and to contend with pride;
> When grieved, to pray; when injured, to forgive,
> And with the world in charity to live.

From these and other references, there could be little doubt as to his fitness and natural piety. Besides, he knew the Scriptures intimately, and thanks to his mother, had been well grounded in the faith. But like other medical students he admitted spending many gay moments over a bottle of wine; and during those amusement spells is said to have composed some witty and significant though ribald lines. For instance:

> With Andrew Collett we the year begin,
> The blind, fat landlord of the old Crown Inn—
> Big as his butt, and, for the self-same use,
> To take in stores of strong fermenting juice.
> On his huge chair beside the fire he sate,
> In revel chief, and umpire in debate;
> Each night his string of vulgar tales he told,
> When ale was cheap and bachelors were bold.
>
> .   .   .   .
>
> On death like his, what names shall we bestow,
> So very sudden ! Yet so very slow !
> 'Twas slow. Disease, augmenting year by year,
> Show'd the grim King by gradual steps brought near;
> 'Twas not less sudden; in the night he died,
> He drank, he swore, he jested, and he lied;
> Thus aiding folly with departing breath,
> Beware, Lorenzo, the slow, sudden death.[1]

Bearing in mind the young man's real repentance, and knowing him as we do, can there be any surprise when Mr. Crabbe, having passed a very creditable examination, was admitted to Deacon's Orders in London on December 21st, 1781, by Dr. Young, Bishop of Norwich, who ordained him a priest in the following August at his own cathedral ? Having been ordained thus, he went with a title to the curacy at St. Peter and St. Paul's Church, Aldeburgh. It would appear from enquiry that the Rev. James Bennett had been the parish rector for over twenty years, and should, therefore, know how to write the most important testimonial in the student's favour, required then, as now, by the Bishop of the Diocese. "And what, it will naturally be

---

[1] " The Parish Register."

asked, was his reception by the people," says the biographer, " when he reappeared among them in this new character?" He replies: " The prophet is not without honour save in his own country." Everybody affirmed that the man who failed as a doctor could not succeed as a parson. Indeed, they questioned whether this poverty-stricken rhymester should be permitted to officiate in sacred matters at all. They were used to—

> A rich young creature, who, they say, is cross'd
> In love, and has in part his senses lost,
> His health for certain, and he comes to spend
> His time with us; we hope our air will mend
> A frame so weaken'd, for the learned tribe
> A change of air for stubborn ills prescribe,
> And doing nothing often has prevail'd
> When ten physicians have prescribed and fail'd.

Little wonder, then, that old Captain Groome's daughters should say with that refined air as they smoothed their black mittens, " We never thought much of Mr. Crabbe."[1] Still, though coldly received officially, it is not unnatural to suppose that the young deacon felt rather elated after his recent literary successes, and with promises of higher appointments would think very little about " unfriendly countenances " and unkind remarks. He valued more than anything else during these few months his nearness to dear Myra, who, we are told, " prudently resisted every proposition of immediate marriage until her lover should have reached some position less precarious than that of a mere curate." What could be done, then, to hasten matters?

> He once had hope—hope, ardent, lively, light—
> His feelings pleasant and his prospects bright:
> Eager of fame, he read, he thought, he wrote,
> Weigh'd the Greek page and added note on note.

[1] *Two Suffolk Friends.*

> At morn, at evening, at his work was he,
> And dreamed what his Euripides would be.[1]

The second clerical examination over, now would
be the time to remind those influential and distinguished friends in London that he had, to use the
Lord Chancellor's own words, " made himself capable
of preferment." Soon afterwards Mr. Burke wrote,
saying he had been speaking to the Duke of Rutland
about him, as his Grace needed a domestic chaplain
to succeed the Rev. George Turner, Rector of Knipton,
who wished to resign his duties for reasons of health;
should such an appointment appeal to him, perhaps
Mr. Crabbe could come up to town and he would be
pleased to make arrangements for an interview. This
letter arrived when the curate happened to be spending
a few days at Parham with Mrs. Elmy's relatives and
her daughter. How did the lovers receive it ? The
news, though startling, must have been welcome, for
he had no hesitation in accepting the invitation. Still,
there were the recollections of Cheveley Park and the
poem so largely connected with that epoch in George's
life, only seven years ago, when he had published such
rash couplets as—

> The King, who nods upon his rattle throne,
> The staggering Peer, to midnight revel prone;
> Lo ! proud Flaminius, at the splendid board,
> The easy chaplain of an atheist lord,
> Quaffs the bright juice with all the gust of sense,
> And clouds his brain in torpid elegance.

Besides, the Crabbes were Liberals, so there would be
political differences. Yes, but in spite of everything,
Burke became all-powerful with the Duke, who felt
that a young author would be a valuable acquisition
to the society of his mansion. Accordingly, in the
following November (1782), the poet took up the
chaplain's quarters at Belvoir.

[1] " The Borough Curate."

BELVOIR CASTLE, C. 1700.

AND AFTER 1800—
"WHEN LO! ANOTHER CASTLE ROSE IN VIEW."
Crabbe.   facing p. 25.

CHAPTER IV

BELVOIR CASTLE AND THE CHAPLAINCY

> Now could he look on that delightful place,
> The glorious dwelling of a princely race. . . .
> Beauty and grandeur were within; around
> Lawn, wood, and water; the delicious ground
> Had parks where deer disport, and game abound.

CRABBE lived in the large, flat, one-storied, oblong building, which then possessed so few distinguished architectural features as belong to the present mediæval looking fortress rebuilt after a fire in 1816. Still, it had charms, and he knew both quite well. Therefore, judging from the above description of " Belvoir[1] Castle," jotted down on arrival, and another written thirty years later, the writer admired most things connected with it at all times, especially the situation and surroundings. True, we admit exceptions, but have no direct information as to the causes, perhaps best expressed by these lines:

> Think you, my Lord, your Belvoir heights infuse
> Vigour, like old Parnassus, to the Muse ?
> Not so: Parnassus was a dismal scene,
> And hunger made the wretched Tenants keen.

However, the biographer merely says: " I have heard my father mention but few occurrences in this period of his life, and if I had, the privacy of a family is not to be invaded because of its public station." Nevertheless, he adds: " The numberless allusions to the nature of a literary dependent's existence in a great lord's house, found in the writings, and especially in the tale of ' The Patron,' go to prove that it was attended with

---

[1] Ancient spelling—Bellevoire: pronounced " Beevor."

many painful circumstances." So long as the chaplain chanced to be alone with the Duke, " a generous man, cordial, frank, and free," ready " to converse on literary topics, quote verses, and criticise plays," either here or in Croxton Park when fishing, he was in his element, but unfortunately these were only occasional privileges, soon cut short by his Grace's appointment to the Lord-Lieutenancy of Ireland. The official position of a clergyman in the Church of England amongst both the guests and, above all, their servants, wounded the youthful cleric's pride. The late chaplain, the Rev. F. W. Knox, discussing the point with the writer, summed up very aptly the tradition of the establishment in these few words: " They teased him." Hence the following reference:

> Thou art religion's advocate; take heed
> Hurt not the cause thy pleasure 'tis to plead.
> Men gay and noisy will o'erwhelm thy sense,
> Then loudly laugh at truth's and thy expense;
> While the kind ladies will do all they can
> To check their mirth, and cry, " The good young man !"[1]

Besides, resulting from his politics, the parson had " more than once to drink a glass of salt water because he refused to join in Tory toasts." After these little pleasantries, we are not at all surprised to read, " He was sometimes tempted to wish to exchange his station for a much more humble dwelling," and in this mood he once composed these simple lines:

> Oh ! had I but a little hut,
> That I might hide my head in,
> Where never guest might dare molest
> Unwelcome or unbidden;
> I'd take the jokes of other folks,
> And mine should then succeed 'em,
> Nor would I chide a little pride,
> Or heed a little freedom.

[1] " The Patron."

The most memorable event concerned the long-delayed marriage; for all obstacles now had been removed, and the chaplain went to spend a few weeks at Beccles previous to the ceremony. The registers contain the following entry: " George Crabbe, clerk, of this parish, single man, and Sarah Elmy, of the same, single woman, were married in this church by licence from the Chancellor, this fifteenth day of December, 1783, by me, P. Routh, curate." Thus ended very happily the engagement of eleven years. The bride and bridegroom lost no time in going into residence. The rooms were close to the present chapel, and may be seen in a model of the old building, still preserved in the picture gallery. Here, however, they remained little more than a year after the Duke left, because, " although there were many obvious advantages to a couple of narrow income in this position, and the noble owner of the seat had given the most strict orders that their convenience should be consulted in every possible manner by his servants, it was soon found to be a disagreeable thing to inhabit the house and be attended by the domestics of an absent family."

For various reasons Mr. Crabbe did not accompany the Duke to Dublin. Being still under thirty, apparently not ambitious for ecclesiastical preferment, like an Irish Bishopric, but rather anxious to accede to his wife's wishes, he decided to remain behind. Mrs. Crabbe, on her part, felt reluctant to go so far whilst her mother lived, and family affairs required attention. Besides, both had a very great longing to settle down in their own English country home within an easy reach of Suffolk. In this respect the chaplain's abode served their purpose until something more suitable could be found. Meanwhile, clerical duties becoming light, the poet produced a considerable amount of his best literary work in this delightful spot, but some parts undoubtedly had been commenced previously. It included the obituary notice on the heroic death of Lord Robert Manners, commander of H.M.S. *Resolution*, April 12th, 1782, a dignified and exemplary prose composition, found in *The Annual Register* of the following year, and two poems. With regard to the first of these, Boswell gives the judgment of one who counts, and incidentally affords a clue to the exact date of authorship, by stating, under "Sunday, March 23rd, 1783": "Soon after this I had an opportunity of seeing, by means of one of his friends, a proof that his talents, as well as his obliging service to authors, were ready as ever. He (the Doctor) had revised 'The Village,' an admirable poem by the Reverend Mr. Crabbe. Its sentiments as to the false notions of rustic happiness and rustic virtue were quite congenial with his own; and he had taken the trouble not only to suggest slight corrections and variations, but to furnish some lines when he thought he could give the writer's meaning better than in the words of the manuscript." He also took care to add: "I must, however, observe that the aids he gave to this poem, as to 'The Traveller' and 'Deserted Village' of Goldsmith, were so small as by no means to impair the distinguishing merit of the author."[1] And, owing to the absence of a preface to this book, there is no other direct evidence as from whence it was written except the concluding address to his Grace:

> Grief is a foe—expel him then thy soul,
> Let nobler thoughts the nearer views control;
> Oh! make the age to come thy better care,
> See other Rutlands, other Granbys there;
> And, as thy thoughts through streaming ages glide,
> See other heroes die as Manners died.

Concerning the second poem, entitled "The Newspaper," we are informed that the greatest part was written at Belvoir soon after the dissolution of Parlia-

[1] *Life of Johnson.*

ment in March, 1784, and just before the coming election, when Mr. Crabbe had been moved to take up the subject by the indignation he felt on seeing Mr. Burke daily abused at " this busy bustling time " by one set of party writers, while the Duke of Rutland was equally the victim of another. The political atmosphere, indeed, did not seem to be dissimilar altogether from our own day, nearly one hundred and fifty years afterwards, with its highly debatable problems of more highways, derating, and unemployment.

> But, oh ! ye muses, keep your votary's feet
> From tavern haunts where politicians meet,
> Where rector, doctor, and attorney pause,
> First on each parish, then each public cause,
> Indited roads and rates that still increase,
> The murmuring poor, who will not fast in peace.
> Election zeal and friendship, since declined,
> A tax commuted, or a tithe in kind;
> The Dutch and Germans kindling into strife,
> Dull port and poachers vile;—the ills of life—
> Here comes the neighbouring Justice pleased to guide
> His little club and in the chair preside.
> In private business his commands prevail,
> On public themes his reasoning turns the scale:
> Assenting silence soothes his happy ear,
> And, in or out, his party triumphs here.

The chaplaincy does, to some extent, mark another phase in the poet's career, because from now onwards " the duties of a pastor " were rendered faithfully in accordance with the eighteenth-century custom, and afforded him so many of those personal experiences which he characteristically illustrated afterwards in " The Parish Register," " The Borough," and " The Tales." The correspondence, however, between the chaplain and the Duke extracted by the Historical MSS. Commission contains these significant lines, dated " 1784, August, Belvoir ":

> I (and I thank your Grace) have ceased to strive
> For niggard rhymes that keep us just alive,
> And little care if now it pleased the State
> To tax your poets as they tax your plate:
> Exempt from both, my useless life I'd close,
> Use humbler ware, and correspond in prose.

We know he had won fame through " The Village," but little profit accrued so far from the book's sale. Quite probably, then, Mr. and Mrs. Crabbe had between them arrived at the conclusion that their financial position was too precarious after marriage, and sought measures to secure further ecclesiastical emolument. For the biographer informs us that a reminder had been sent to that exalted friend in London about his promise of Crown patronage; so the chaplain received an invitation to dine with Lord Thurlow—" and this is another of those incidents in his life which," the son says, " I much regret that he himself has given no account of, for I should suppose many expressions characteristic of the rough old Chancellor might have been recorded. My father only said that before he left the house his noble host told him that ' By G—— he was as like " Parson Adams " as twelve to a dozen,' and gave him the small livings of Frome St. Quintin and Evershot, in Dorsetshire, worth about £200, and a rectory (March, 1783)." But before deciding to reside there, George and Myra went over to see the place. And since it happened to be a long and tiring journey by the old stage coaches, they came to the conclusion that Dorset was much too far from Suffolk family ties. How, then, were they to act? They would be wanting in prudence to refuse what had been accepted, or to resign the present appointment, even although the quarters were not altogether desirable. The rector-designate solved the problem by taking upon himself the responsibility for the cure of souls in those joint parishes, and appointing the Rev. Nathaniel Bartlett to act as his curate-in-charge.

Simple he was, and loved the simple truth,
Yet had some useful cunning from his youth,
A cunning never to dishonour lent.
And rather for defence than conquest meant;
He ever aimed to please, and to offend
Was ever cautious, for he sought a friend.

Eighteen months later he and his wife were existing largely upon this source of income at the Castle. The " something additional," however, soon afterwards turned up; because Dr. Thomas Parke, Archdeacon of Stamford as well as Rector of Stathern, required a *locum tenens* for that parish and, accordingly, engaged the Rev. George Crabbe.

Old cottages, landmarks, and foundations indicate a very compact village, hedged in on two sides by the Belvoir woods and the Harby hills. The locality appears fascinating when viewed from the distant terrace heights above, but is really dull and flat and not altogether healthy in winter owing to swampy ground. So we are soon informed that the cunning minister took the precaution of asking the Duke's favour to return to his old quarters should he be troubled with " agues and impassable roads."

The pretty Early English Church of St. Guthlac still looks the same with two distinguished weather-beaten porches on the north and south sides respectively. It possesses some trifling archæological features such as an ancient Saxon stone, which fills one of the angles of the outside walls, together with Consecration Crosses—small, deeply incised, and reputed to have been blessed by Hugh, the saintly Bishop of Lincoln, and also a well-preserved thirteenth-century chantry now used as organ chamber and vestry. The interior, however, underwent restoration in the early forties of last century, and that rather drastic process has altered the appearance considerably. Still the beautiful font of the Decorated period in which the poet baptised three of his children can be seen.

But much old woodwork has gone with the high pews, and a new stone pulpit occupies the site of the former three-decker.

There, just beyond the churchyard and in full prospect of the tower, stands the large and lofty double-fronted Rectory, where the biographer was born. Here he lived for four years with his parents, and informs us: " My father often said they were, on the whole, the very happiest in his life. My mother and he could now ramble together at their ease amidst the rich woods of Belvoir without any of the painful feelings which had before chequered his enjoyment of the place: at home a garden afforded him healthful exercise and unfailing amusement. . . . At Stathern, and all his successive country residences, he continued to practise his original profession among such poor people as chose to solicit his aid. The contents of his medicine chest, and, among the rest, cordials, were ever at their service; he grudged no personal fatigue to attend the sick-bed of the peasant in the double capacity of physician and priest." With regard to clerical duty we may justly infer that he strove earnestly, if unsuccessfully, to improve the morals of his younger parishioners. There is a tradition handed down by a former incumbent (the Rev. J. W. Taylor) to the effect that when a youthful couple wished to be married they were driven from the church with the remark that he (Crabbe, the officiating minister) had come there to marry " men and women, and not lads and wenches !" But the truth is more likely to be found in the following lines under " Marriages—a Parish Wedding ":

> Next at our Altar stood a luckless pair,
> Brought by strong passions and a warrant there;
> By long rent cloak, hung loosely, strove the bride,
> From every eye, what all perceived, to hide.
> While the boy-bridegroom, shuffling in his pace,
> Now hid awhile and then exposed his face;

As shame, alternately with anger strove,
The brain confused with muddy ale, to move
In haste, and stammering he perform'd his part,
And look'd the rage that rankled in his heart
(So will each lover only curse his fate,
Too soon made happy and made wise too late);
I saw his features take a savage gloom
And deeply threaten for the days to come.
Low spake the lass, and lisp'd and minced the while,
Look'd on the lad, and faintly tried to smile.
With soften'd speech and humble tone she strove
To stir the embers of departed love;
While he, a tyrant, frowning walked before,
Felt the poor purse, and sought the public door,
She sadly following, in submission went
And saw the final shilling foully spent.
Then to her father's hut the pair withdrew,
And bade to love and comfort long adieu !
Ah ! fly temptation, youth, refrain ! refrain !
I preach for ever; but I preach in vain ![1]

[1] " The Parish Register."

CHAPTER V

THE BELVOIR NATURALIST: A LOCAL CHARACTER AND THE STORY OF A FOUNDLING

One morn, I rambled, thinking of the past,
Far in the country.   Did you ever fast
Through a long summer's day ? or, sturdy, go
To pluck the crab, the bramble, and the sloe,
The hip, the cornel, and the beech, the food
And the wild solace of the gypsy brood ?
To pick the cress embrown'd by summer sun,
From the dry bed where streams no longer run ?
Have you, like school-boy, mingling play and toil,
Dug for the ground-nut, and enjoy'd the spoil ?
Or chafed with feverish hand the ripening wheat,
Resolved to fast, and yet compelled to eat ?

FROM the first to the last day in his chaplaincy Crabbe paid diligent attention to all the surrounding beauties of Nature, and in this connection botany as a study always afforded him much pleasure.   Indeed, he would occasionally sally forth alone to explore the country long before breakfast and, we are told, " out of doors he had always some object in view—a flower or a pebble, or his notebook in his hand. He read aloud very often, even when walking or seated by the side of his wife in the huge old-fashioned one-horse chaise, heavier than a modern chariot, in which they usually were conveyed in their little excursions, and the conduct of which he, from awkwardness and absence of mind, prudently relinquished to my mother on all occasions."   Rare plants and herbs discovered in this way for miles around were carefully transferred to his garden or to the study for microscopical investigations, and afterwards systematically tabulated.   This scien-

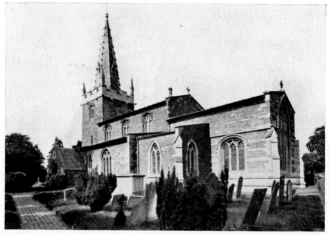

Photo.   Alfred Newton, Leicester.

BRANSTON-BY-BELVOIR CHURCH.

Photo.   Alfred Newton, Leicester.

LAKE VIEW.

facing p. 35.

tific work became known just when Nichols, the county
historian, started collecting material. He, therefore,
asked Mr. Crabbe to contribute the results of his
research into the fauna, flora, and fossils of the Vale of
Belvoir, and that treatise is found in the first of four
volumes published in 1795. In one of the " Tales "
we get further particulars concerning that pleasant
hobby in Myra's company at this time such as:

> The very lane has sweets that all admire;
> The rambling suckling and the vigorous brier;
> See ! Wholesome wormwood grows beside the way,
> Where dew press'd yet the dog-rose bends the spray;
> Fresh the herbs, the fields, fair shrubs the banks adorn,
> And snow-white bloom falls flaky from the thorn.
> No fostering hand they need, no sheltering wall,
> They spring uncultured, and they bloom for all.[1]

So let us picture mentally a roundabout excursion
at the end of June, or a little later, starting from
Stathern towards the Knipton Reservoir. There the
naturalist would leave his young wife to look after the
gig whilst he searched the low boggy ground at and
near Branston, where sometimes the tiny Devon stream
seemed almost to cease flowing. After a fresh start
they quickly entered the Park for lunch. Then,
climbing the dry Croxton banks close to the church
in search for the " common birdsfoot," the route
would be continued through the Harston lane.

> Onward he went, and fiercer grew the heat,
> Dust rose in clouds before the horse's feet.

Then along the road to Woolsthorpe, when the following observation is recorded upon the " Listera Ovata ":
" The name commemorates Dr. Martin Lister, con-
temporary with Ray, best known as a conchologist and
entomologist."

In the cool of the evening they return home across

[1] " The Lover's Journey."

the Castle grounds and over the Belvoir plantations, which had only recently inspired him with this simile on the heroic death of Lord Robert:

> As the tall oak, whose vigorous branches form
> An ample shade, and brave the wildest storm,
> High o'er the subject wood is seen to grow,
> The guard and glory of the trees below,
> Till on its head the fiery bolt descends,
> And o'er the plain the shattered trunk extends;
> Yet then it lies all wondrous as before,
> And still the glory, though the guard no more;
> So thou, when every virtue, every grace,
> Rose in thy soul, or shone within thy face
> When, though the son of Granby, thou wert known
> Less by thy father's glory than thy own.

Pleasant jaunts like these could only be indulged in now and again, for three children were born at the parsonage and baptised between November 16th, 1785, and January 23rd, 1789. We are also informed about the mother's rather delicate health. Moreover, it must not be too readily supposed that Mrs. Crabbe, even metaphorically speaking, drove her husband " on all occasions " from pillar to post. Suffice it to say Mr. Crabbe always took the reins himself when on horseback. Then he often visited Goadby Marwood, a small parish situated about six miles away, not only to seek rare floral specimens in the sandy pits at Piper Hole, but to call on Dr. Edmund Cartwright, the eminent incumbent, poet, scientist, and mechanic, who occasionally stayed here at the Rectory; for he lived chiefly—

> In a large town, a wealthy thriving place,
> Where hopes of gain excite an anxious race;
> Which dark dense wreaths of cloudy volumes cloak,
> And mark, for leagues around, the place of smoke;
> Where fire to water lends its powerful aid,
> And steam produces—strong ally to trade.

There vast machines were worked under his direction. "Few persons could tell a story so well; no man could make more of a trite one." We can, therefore, well imagine these two friends having much in common, informing each other of all the notable circumstances in their respective experience. The Crabbes also went to stay with the Cartwrights, at Doncaster, and were much impressed at the sight of the engines "thundering with resistless power." Then, seemingly, the houses of the industrial magnates would be pointed out, accompanied by anecdotes concerning this and that person's career.

So the theory that our poet owes to Goadby the conception of a few typical "tales" amongst the many preserved for publication at a later period is most likely to be correct. One concerns a "Foundling":

> To name an infant meet our village sires
> Assembled all as such event requires.
> Frequent and full the rural sages sate,
> And speakers many urged the long debate.
> Some hardened knaves who roved the country round
> Had left a babe within the parish bound.
> First, of the fact they questioned—"Was it true?"
> The child was brought. What then remained to do?
> "Was't dead or living?" This was fairly proved:
> 'Twas pinched—it roared, and every doubt removed.
> Then by what names th' unwelcome guest to call
> Was long a question; and it posed them all;
> For he who lent it to a babe unknown,
> Censorious men might take it for his own.
> They looked about, they gravely spoke to all,
> And not one Richard answered to the call.
> Next they enquired the day when, passing by,
> Th' unlucky peasant heard the stranger's cry.
> This known, how food and raiment they might give
> Was next debated, for the rogue would live.
> At last, with all their words and work content,
> Back to their homes the prudent vestry went,
> And Richard Monday to the Workhouse sent,
> There was he pinch'd and pitied, thump'd and fed,

And duly took his beatings and his bread;
Patient in all control, in all abuse,
He found contempt and kicking have their use:
Sad, silent, supple; bending to the blow,
A slave of slaves, the lowest of the low.

.   .   .   .

He rose in favour, when in fame he fell;
Base was his usage, vile his whole employ,
And all despised and fed the pliant boy.
At length, " 'Tis time he should abroad be sent,"
Was whispered near him,—and abroad he went;
One morn they call'd him, Richard answer'd not;
They deem'd him hanging, and in time forgot,—
Yet miss'd him long, as each, throughout the clan,
Found he " had better spared a better man."
Now Richard's talents for the world were fit,
He'd no small cunning, and had some small wit,
Had that calm look which seemed to all assent,
And that complacent speech which nothing meant,
He'd but one care, and that he strove to hide—
How best for Richard Monday to provide !
Steel through opposing plates the magnet draws,
And steely atoms culls from dust and straws;
And thus our hero, to his interest true,
Gold through all bars and from each trifle drew.
And still more surely round the world to go
This fortune's child had neither friend nor foe.
Long lost to us, at last our man we trace—
" Sir Richard Monday died at Monday-place."
His lady's worth, his daughter's, we peruse,
And find his grandsons all as rich as Jews.
He gave reforming charities a sum,
And bought the blessings of the blind and dumb,
Bequeathed to missions money from the stocks,
And Bibles issued from his private box;
But to his native place, severely just,
He left a pittance, bound in rigid trust—
Two paltry pounds, on every quarter's-day
(At Church produced), for forty loaves should pay.
A stinted gift, that to the parish shows
He kept in mind their bounty—and their blows ![1]

[1] " The Parish Register."

During the chaplaincy the poet had ample opportunity and time also to study the prevailing conditions
among both rich and poor. Hitherto, his observation
and actual experience had been confined chiefly to the
lower classes. Now, in Leicestershire, he could compare the sad lot of the agricultural labourer with the
gay huntsman of the Melton Mowbray district, then,
as now, numbering some of the richest folk in England,
and that at a time when wealth was far less evenly
distributed. Indeed, the following lines are recorded
just to illustrate the difference between the eighteenth
and twentieth centuries in these respects:

> When plenty smiles—alas ! she smiles for few—
> And those who taste not, yet behold her store,
> Are as the slaves that dig the golden ore—
> The wealth around them makes them doubly poor.
> Or will you deem them amply paid in health,
> Labour's fair child, that languishes with wealth ?
> Go, then, and see them rising with the sun,
> Through a long course of daily toil to run;
> See them beneath the Dog-star's raging heat,
> When the knees tremble and the temples beat;
> Behold them, leaning on their scythes, look o'er
> The labour past, and toils to come explore;
> See them alternate suns and showers engage,
> And hoard up aches and anguish for their age;
> Then own that labour may as fatal be
> To these thy slaves as thine excess to thee.[1]

On this subject a writer in the *Quarterly Review* for
1833 said: " It is good for the proprietor of an estate
to know that such things are, and at his own doors.
He might have guessed, indeed, as a general truth,
even whilst moving in his own exclusive sphere, that
many a story of intense interest might be supplied by
the annals of his parish. Crabbe would have taught
him thus much, had he been a reader of that most
sagacious of observers, most searching of moral

[1] " The Village."

anatomists, most graphic of poets; and we reverence this great writer not less for his genius than for his patriotism, in bravely lifting the veil which is spread between the upper classes and the working-day world, and letting one half of mankind know what the other half is about."

THE PATRON.

facing p. 4¹.

CHAPTER VI

THE PATRON

Great were his gifts, his mighty heart I own,
But why describe what all the world has known ?
The rest is petty pride, the useless art
Of a vain mind to hide a swelling heart.[1]

CHARLES the fourth duke possessed an elevated turn of mind that specially attracted those great statesmen Burke and Pitt, who were instrumental in starting him upon so promising a Parliamentary career, first to represent his University, and next the King in the Lord-Lieutenancy of Ireland. Indeed, from a scholastic point of view, there seems to be no doubt, according to his tutor-professor, afterwards Bishop Watson, " that the world was not conscious of half his worth." Again, more recently, a careful student of political economy has candidly stated " that, but for an early death, his ability might have given him a place in the history of the Empire."[2] But Crabbe's cleverly gifted patron inherited a weakness from his illustrious father perhaps best described in one word—extravagance. He is said to have had a quaint obsession concerning the Manners' property and its value, reputed to be worth then not much more than £25,000 per annum. High living in his splendid Viceregal establishment where " his table presented every delicacy which luxury could accumulate or display," racehorses at Newmarket, foxhounds at Croxton, town houses in London and Dublin, besides several small estates, such as Cheveley and Haddon, to maintain,

[1] " The Borough."
[2] *The English in Ireland*, J. A. Froude.

required something like double that amount to meet just current expenses.   At the outset, when in dire need of his patronage, the poet notes this characteristic. He refers to that " generous friend of ample power possessed," " some noble Rutland, misery's friend and thine," and thus exclaims:

> Go on, then, son of vision !   Still pursue
> Thy airy dreams; the world is dreaming, too,
> Ambition's lofty views, the pomp of State,
> The pride of wealth, the splendour of the great,
> Stripp'd of their mask, their cares and troubles known,
> Are visions far less happy than thy own.

One well-known dream concerned the emoluments of the Crown's chief officials.   According to his fanciful notion, the nation ought to meet all their bills ! Occasionally, however, he felt doubtful with regard to such theories, and endeavoured to curtail both his public and private manner of living.   For it is amusing to note how the reckless spendthrift writes to the Duchess, only four years after their marriage: " You must not purchase everything your eye is attached to, no superfluous clothes beyond that is requisite for you to appear clean and decent."   That the chaplain used his influence in trying to overcome this vicious tendency is obvious again and again in his writings.   Some, indeed, seem to infer that he rather overdid it, hence unpleasantness.

> If never heeded, thy attack is vain;
> And if they heed thee they'll attack again.
> Then, too, in striking at that heedless rate
> Thou in an instant may'st decide thy fate.
> Leave admonition; let the Vicar give
> Rules how the Nobles of his flock should live,
> Nor take that simple fancy to thy brain
> That thou canst cure the wicked and the vain.[1]

[1] " The Patron."

Unfortunately, all attempts to stem the tide, which went on increasing and gathering speed, were unavailing. It is the pace that kills, so, after less than five years' occupancy of this important post, his Excellency passed away on October 24th, 1787, in the thirty-fifth year of his age.

The biographer says: " My father had a strong personal regard for his Grace, and grieved sincerely at the loss of a kind and condescending friend. Had he cherished ambitious views he might have grieved for himself too." So when they brought the embalmed body from Dublin (where it had been lying some time in state) for burial in the family vault at Bottesford, the chaplain preached the commemoration sermon. And as the composition is comparatively free from sentiment and flattery, so clearly expresses the writer's spirit of admiration and gratitude, and at the same time adds much interest to the story, we extract the following passage: " It is most remarkable that one family should afford three individuals so eminently distinguished in so short a period, and those a father and his two sons, a father venerated and almost adored in this nation for his humanity and courage, and celebrated through Europe for his honour and military achievements. So that of every name which this happy kingdom is adorned by, the name of Granby has probably been most universally known and has extorted praise and admiration, even from the foes of, and the strangers to, this country. Of his sons, one endowed with every amiable virtue, talent, and accomplishment fell at an early period in the moment of an important victory which gave life and peace to his nation, death and glory to him. His noble brother a few years survived him, arriving at the highest honours which a subject can enjoy in one kingdom, and being sovereign in another, where he filled the most exalted station in the most critical period with firmness and dignity; and after raising expectation by his virtues and exceeding hope in his success, he died at an age when even among the eminent of mankind talents only begin their promise and our applause, awaiting the decision of time—he died and left to his survivors admiration mingled with grief, together with the reasonable expectation that those who are heirs of his temporal possessions may inherit his virtues also, and leave untarnished to their successors the hereditary glory of their house." When the Rev. George Crabbe, jun., about forty years later began hunting up his father's papers, he happened to come across this manuscript, and after a hasty glance or two somewhat ungraciously dismissed it with the epithet, "A Valueless Sermon"! Strangely enough, it played a part in shaping his future destiny, and is important in refuting unfavourable opinions of strained relationship between the patron and the poet which apparently did not exist. Because from old letters recently discovered, we may more confidently affirm, to the honour of both, that the former took no offence and the latter showed no resentment when the separation came. They continued to communicate with each other, Crabbe in rhyme, and that occasionally far from elegant in sentiment and style. Still these " epistles " reveal a mutual understanding, perhaps best explained by Dale in these words: " Young as they were, each had gained some fame. The Duke was already regarded as a statesman of promise, and the poet had achieved some note by his works. Moreover, they were at a period of life when the attractions of common interests make friendship possible between men of different rank. . . . We may surmise that the choice of the Chaplain's company, for instance, on a hunting day was not only a matter of pleasure, but one of prudence. The man who had the discernment to see under the somewhat uncouth exterior Crabbe's real goodness and ability, would also be able to value intercourse with him, and be ready to avail himself of his poetic insight and ardour, as a means of preparation for the political life on which his ambition was already fixed."[1]   Crabbe could truly express his personal loss by writing that the task is hard—

>   . . . to heal the bleeding heart,
> To bid the still-recurring thoughts depart,
> Tame the fierce grief and stem the rising sigh,
> And curb rebellious passion with reply;
> Calmly to dwell on all that pleased before,
> And yet to know that all shall please no more;—
> To such these thoughts will lasting comfort give,
> Life is not measured by the time we live;
> 'Tis not an even course of three-score years—
> A life of narrow views and paltry fears,
> Grey hairs and wrinkles and the cares they bring,
> That take from Death the terrors or the sting;
> But 'tis the gen'rous spirit, mounting high
> Above the world, that native of the sky;
> Such Manners was, so he resigned his breath . . .
> Cease, then, that grief, and let those tears subside;
> If passion rule us, be that passion pride;
> If reason, reason bids us strive to raise
> Our fallen hearts, and be like him we praise.
> Or if affection still the soul subdue,
> Bring all his virtues, all his worth in view,
> For how can grief so deeply wound the heart,
> When admiration claims so large a part ?

Yes, undoubtedly the patron's premature death sadly affected the poet, so for the moment we leave him in solitude, quietly meditating upon our frail human nature:

> Death levels men—the wicked and the just,
> The wise, the weak, lie blended in the dust;
> And by the honours dealt to every name,
> The King of Terrors seems to level fame.
> —See ! here lamented wives, and every wife
> The pride and comfort of her husband's life;
> Here, too, her spouse, with every virtue graced,
> His mournful widow has a trophy placed.

[1] *History of the Belvoir Hunt.*

CHAPTER VII

CROXTON KERRIAL'S[1] CHARMING SITUATION—THE VIL-
LAGE: ITS CHURCH AND REGISTERS—A BAPTISM,
DEATH AND BURIAL

> The Village Life, and every care that reigns
> O'er youthful peasants and declining swains;
> What form the real pictures of the poor,
> Demand a song—the Muse can give no more.

THE son says with regard to Croxton, " I have heard
my father speak of the relief and pleasure of wandering
through the deep glades and secluded paths of the
woods." So, being no longer attached to the Duke,
Crabbe reviews certain impressions already recorded
during holiday residence within the parish and
enquires:

> Is there a place save one the poet sees—
> A land of love, of liberty, and ease—
> Where labour wearies not, nor cares suppress
> Th' eternal flow of rustic happiness,
> Where no proud mansion frowns in awful state
> Or keeps the sunshine from the cottage gate.
> Where young and old intent on pleasure throng;
> And half man's life is holiday and song ?

He does not tell us the answer, because that might
constitute a challenge; but simply prefers to point
out and give a general description of charming features sufficiently familiar to those who may recognise
them :

> Behold the cot ! where thrives the industrious swain,
> Source of his pride, his pleasure, and his gain;

[1] Ancient spelling—Crokeson and Cyriol : pronounced Croson-
Keriol.

46

Screen'd from the winter's wind, the sun's last ray
Smiles on the window, and prolongs the day;
Projecting thatch the woodbine's branches stop,
And turn their blossoms to the casement top.

Survey the peerless park, with its long winding
carriage drive, and undulating heights crowned by
" Belvoir's lordly towers " several miles away.

Thy walks are very pleasant, every scene
Is rich in beauty, lively or serene—
Rich is that varied view with woods around,
Seen from the seat within the shrubb'ry bound,
Where shines the distant lake, and where appear,
From ruins bolting, unmolested deer.

Look, when arriving from Melton, at that lofty
cluster of dwellings formerly styled a town, as to this
day by " Rose's Town-end," where things are
" lively "—for example, at the " Smithy," the " Peacock Inn," and the Seminary founded in 1711:

The place
Where the good widow schools her infant race,
Shops whence are heard the hammer and the saw,
And village pleasures unreproved by law.
Then how serene, when in your favourite room,
Gales from your jasmines soothe the evening gloom,
When from your upland paddock you look down,
And just perceive the smoke which hides the town.

Cast your eye here and there near the ever running
water spout, and towards the close of day—

When cattle slowly cross the shallow brook,
And shepherds pen their folds and rest upon their crook.

Consult the foresters, and you will hear them say:

We prune our hedges, prime our slender trees
And nothing looks untutored, and at ease,
On the wild heath or in the flowery vale.

These and similar enchantments can hardly be disputed, especially since the Premonstratensian Canons chose a site here for their home in 1162, and they are acknowledged to have had a notable eye for selecting attractive positions. Moreover, after the Belvoir Castle was destroyed during the Civil Wars, it is stated that the " rebuilding took place owing to the wish and taste of the Countess of Rutland, but the Earl himself would have preferred Croxton, where later his grandson built."

However, the chaplain, we may be sure, lost no time in visiting its prominent church. The main historical facts would be already familiar as the result of enquiry at the Castle, whence a good view could be seen. So we need draw attention to a few points only. There seems to have been an older foundation than the present one, dedicated to St. John the Baptist, and given to the Abbot of Croxton by William, Count de Boulogne, son of King Stephen. The exact date is unknown, nevertheless the records state that the monks used the edifice for a long time previous to the Abbey erection; therefore, in any case it must have been before the year last mentioned. The mere fact that one descends from without into the nave confirms the saintly patronage. The massive construction of four large and pointed archways in the lower portion of a central belfry indicates the cruciform plan of a pre-existent structure. But the late Mr. M. H. Bloxam, F.S.A., a well-known Leicestershire archæologist, in his visitation address, July 2nd, 1869, said: " He did not find anything earlier than the fourteenth century, of which period the nave, the tower and doorway in the north aisle were examples. The clerestory was of the fifteenth century, and the walls of side arches were taken down and re-erected at that period." This statement just includes the three styles in architecture called Early English, Decorated, and Perpendicular, or more generally Gothic. What, then, says the poet ?

Photo. *Alfred Newton, Leicester.*

ST. JOHN THE BAPTIST'S CHURCH, CROXTON KERRIAL.

facing p. 48.

> The old foundation—but it is not clear
> When it was laid—you care not for the year;
> Yet Gothic all—the learn'd who visit us
> (And our small wonders) have decided thus:
> " Yon noble Gothic arch," " That Gothic door,"
> So have they said; of proof you'll need no more.
> Here large plain columns rise in solemn style,
> You'd love the gloom they make in either aisle.

On nearing the precincts of its nave, famed far and wide for beautiful fifteenth-century monastic bench-end carvings, a pleasing feature is the south porch. This contains what remains of the holy water stoup and niche over the archway for the patron saint, both damaged in the Civil Wars, since many bullets have been found embedded in the leaden roofs above. He then proceeds:

> But ere you enter, yon bold tower survey,
> Tall and entire, and venerably grey.
> For time has soften'd what was harsh when new,
> And now the stains are all of sober hue.

We are next informed that after several centuries' wear and tear it

> . . . yet stands, and has its bells renown'd
> For size magnificent and solemn sound;
> Each has its motto; some contrived to tell,
> In monkish rhyme, the uses of a bell.

Indeed, three of the six are thus inscribed: " Merorem mestis letis sic leta sonabo," " I will sound sadness to the sad and joy to the joyful," dated 1613; " Sancta Maria," " Holy Mary," a reminder of the days when the " Angelus " rang morning, noon, and night; and " Cælorum Christe placeat tibi Rex Sonus Iste," " May this sound please Thee, O Christ, King of Heaven." In a quaintly-humoured fashion, then, he, or rather the sexton, tells:

5

'Tis a tall building with a tower and bells,
Where priest and clerk with joint exertion strive
To keep the ardour of their flock alive:
That by its periods eloquent and grave,
This by responses and a well set stave.
These for the living; but when life be fled,
I toll myself the requiem for the dead.

Now, if these observations were jotted down after officiating at evensong, we might very fittingly conclude with a passing reference to some such happy cottagers, as, having returned from church, are standing close to their garden gate.

          . . . near the cot,
The reed fence rises round some fav'rite spot,
Where rich carnations, pinks with purple eyes,
Proud hyacinths, the least some florist's prize,
Tulips tall-stemmed and pounced auriculas rise.
Here on a Sunday, we, when service ends,
All speak aloud, are happy and are free,
And glad they seem, and gaily they agree.
Where still the welcome and the words are old,
And the same stories are for ever told;
Yet theirs is joy that bursting from the heart,
Prompts the glad tongue these nothings to impart;
That talks, or laughs, or runs, or shouts, or plays,
And speaks in all their looks and all their ways.

On a similar visit the chaplain would seek an opportunity to inspect what often used to be called " the poor man's charter." Indeed, these very records appear to have suggested the title, and supplied the material for many incidents in the poem entitled " The Parish Register," which contains little pictures and familiar objects in the locality similar to samples already quoted. Moreover, they are often associated with striking individual portraits or family groups sketched in happy satire, according to facts revealed in the parchments. Now it is interesting to note that no regular parochial entries concerning the chief events in ordinary community life are to be found in this country previous to the latter half of the sixteenth century. The monastic records were the oldest, referring chiefly to the clergy and nobility; but when these institutions were dissolved, nearly all the ancient documents perished, greatly to the distress of many families. Cromwell tried to make amends in 1538 by issuing an injunction that every parson, vicar, or curate should keep one book or register wherein to write the day and year of each wedding, christening, and burial made within the parish, etc. Owing to Parliamentary and constitutional changes, twenty years passed before the Protector's order received attention. Croxton Kerrial then, with other parishes in the neighbourhood, came more or less into line, some recording one thing, some another—usually matrimonial events to prevent clandestine wedlock. The majority, however, refrained until compelled by judicial pressure. Thus, we find the Rector and Churchwardens of Bottesford were commanded to appear at Leicester, on "the 10th day of June, in the year of our Lord, 1575 . . ." where they inform us that "we showed our register book, and wanted 23 years." It is also stated that the register begins here in 1621, but that is by no means correct. Phillimore, in his revision, says: "The sheets are for the most part arranged without any regard for chronology. The marriages begin in 1558, the burials in 1559, and the baptisms in 1620." Afterwards the order with dates is regular to the time when the chaplain made his inspection. What impression, we may ask, did it leave upon his mind?

In thinking over the natural sequence of spiritual progress, would he not start with the font and finish at the grave? And, recalling a name connected with each link, especially when it happened to be the first in its section, how could he better express the mental image than by these lines:

Here, with an infant, joyful sponsors came,
Then bear the new-made Christian to its home;
A few short years and we behold him stand
To ask a blessing, with his bride in hand;
A few, still seeming shorter, and we hear
His widow weeping at her husband's bier.

To the reader's mind there appeared little need for
fuller information:

No muse, I ask, before my view to bring,
The humble actions of the swains, I sing—
How passed the youthful, how old their days,
Who sank in sloth, and who aspired to praise;
Their tempers, manners, morals, customs, arts;
What parts they had, and how they 'mploy'd their parts;
By what elated, soothed, seduced, depress'd,
Full well I know—these records give the rest.

For instance, from the earliest recorded marriage, that
between "Robert Tipping and Elizabeth Beckingham,
10th Nov., 1558," and other entries referring to the
same family, such as a recent baptism, the poet is able
to give some praiseworthy description of the then
well-known Croxton tenant-farmer and his wife. To
the font, he says,

. . . with their boy, a decent couple came,
And called him Robert, 'twas his father's name;
Blest in each other, but to no excess,
Health, quiet, comfort form'd their happiness;
Love, all made up of torture and delight,
Was but mere madness in this couple's sight.
Few were their acres—but with these content,
They were each pay-day ready with their rent;
And few their wishes—what their farm denied,
The neighbouring town, at trifling cost, supplied.
If at the draper's window Susan cast
A longing look, as with her goods she pass'd,
And with the produce of the wheel and churn,
Bought her a Sunday-robe on her return,

True to her maxim, she would take no rest,
Till care repaid that portion to the chest;
Or if, when loitering at the Whitsun fair,
Her Robert spent some idle shillings there,
Up at the barn, before the break of day,
He made his labour for the indulgence pay;
Thus both—that waste itself might work in vain
Wrought double tides, and all was well again.
Yet, though so prudent, there were times of joy
(The day they wed; the christening of the boy)
When to the wealthier farmers there was shown
Welcome unfeign'd, and plenty like their own;
For Susan served the great, and had some pride
Among our topmost people to preside;
Yet, in that plenty, in that welcome free,
There was the guiding nice frugality
That, in the festal, as the frugal day,
Has, in a different mode, a Sovereign's sway,
As tides the same attractive influence show,
In the least ebb and in their proudest flow;
The wise frugality, that does not give
A life to saving, but that saves to live;
Sparing, not pinching, mindful though not mean,
O'er all presiding, yet in nothing seen.

Having completed his inspection and taken a walk
round he soliloquised thus:

When these, my records, I reflecting read,
And find what ills these numerous births succeed,
What powerful griefs these nuptial ties attend;
With what regret these painful journeys end,
When, from the cradle to the grave, I look,
Mine, I conceive, a melancholy book.

Then we are given two pictures to illustrate this
conception. The first concerns the sudden death
of "The Widow Goe," who had possibly rented
"Blackwell Lodge" not so far from the heath, and
styled

. . . an active dame,
Famed ten miles round, and worthy all her fame:
She lost her husband when their loves were young,
But kept her farm, her credit and her tongue;
Full thirty years she ruled, with matchless skill,
With guiding judgment and resistless will,
Advice she scorn'd, rebellions she suppressed,
And sons and servants bow'd at her behest.
Her maidens told she was all eye and ear,
In darkness saw, and could at distance hear;
No parish-business in the place could stir,
Without direction or assent from her.
In turn she took each office as it fell
Knew all their duties, and discharged them well;
She look'd on want with judgment clear and cool,
And felt with reason and bestow'd by rule;
She match'd both sons and daughters to her mind,
And lent them eyes, for Love, she heard, was blind;
Yet ceaseless still she throve alert, alive,
The working bee in full or empty hive;
Busy and careful like that working bee,
No time for love nor tender care had she,
But when the farmers made their amorous vows,
She talk'd of market-steeds and patent ploughs,
When, as the busy days of spring drew near,
That call'd for all the forecast of the year;
When lively hope the rising crops survey'd,
And April promised what September paid;
When stray'd her lambs where gorse and greenwood grow,
When rose her grass in richer vales below,
When pleas'd she looked on all the smiling land,
And view'd the hinds who wrought at her command
(Poultry in groups still follow'd where she went),
Then dread o'ercame her—that her days were spent,
" Bless me !   I die, and not a warning giv'n,
With much to do on earth, and all for heav'n !
No reparation for my soul's affairs,
No leave petition'd for the barn's repairs;
Accounts perplex'd, my interest yet unpaid,
My mind unsettled, and my will unmade;
A lawyer haste, and, in your way, a priest,
And let me die in one good work at least."

She spake, and, trembling, dropp'd upon her knees,
Heaven in her eye and in her hand her keys,
And still the more she found her life decay,
With greater force she grasp'd those signs of sway,
Then fell and died !   In haste her sons drew near,
And dropp'd, in haste, the tributary tear;
Then, from the adhering clasp, the keys unbound,
And consolation for their sorrows found.

The other pictures the funeral of

" A valued Mother and a faithful Wife."

And, in this story's narration we get a good insight
into the poet's usual practice of telling the particulars
to an imaginary friend.[1]   Besides, owing to the incumbent's non-residence—the Rev. Anthony Shaw lived
at Stonesby—he probably officiated himself.

Slowly they bore with solemn step the dead;
When grief grew loud and bitter tears were shed,
My part began; a crowd drew near the place,
Awe in each eye, alarm in every face:
So swift the ill, and of so fierce a kind,
That fear with pity mingled with each mind;
Friends with the husband came their griefs to blend;
For good man Frankford was to all a friend.
The last born boy they held above the bier,
He knew not grief, but cries express'd his fear;
Each different age and sex reveal'd its pain,
In now a louder, now a lower strain;
While the meek father, listening to their tones,
Swell'd the full cadence of the grief by groans.
The elder sister strove her pangs to hide
And soothing words to younger minds applied.
" Be still, be patient," oft she strove to say
But fail'd as oft, and weeping turn'd away.
Curious and sad upon the fresh-dug hill
The village lads stood melancholy still;
And idle children, wandering to and fro,
As Nature guided, took the tone of woe.

[1] See Appendix II., p. 180.

Arrived at home, how then they gazed around,
On every place—where she no more was found:—
The seat at table she was wont to fill;
The fire-side chair, still set, but vacant still,
The garden-walks, a labour all her own,
The latticed bower, with trailing shrubs o'ergrown,
The Sunday-pew she fill'd with all her race,
Each place of hers was now a sacred place.
That, while it call'd up sorrows in the eyes,
Pierced the full heart and forced them still to rise.
Oh sacred sorrow ! by whom souls are tried,
Sent not to punish mortals but to guide:
If thou art mine (and who shall proudly dare
To tell his Maker he has had his share ?)
Still let me feel for what thy pangs were sent,
And be my guide, and not my punishment.

CHAPTER VIII

CROXTON'S LOWLY DWELLINGS AND AN EXCEPTION

> Fair scenes of peace ! Ye might detain us long,
> But vice and misery now demand the song.
>
> .　　　.　　　.　　　.
>
> Then, leaving these to their accustomed way,
> The seat itself demands a short delay.
> And if the eye be robbed of half its sight,
> Th' imagination feels the more delight.[1]

FEW signs remain to recall to mind really " old cots "
for the poor at Croxton in Crabbe's time. They would
be sixteenth-century timber-framed huts, with those
other more substantial stone-walled, thatched little
domiciles, later in date, still found here and there about
the village. The majority were narrow, low, and
mean in their general construction, and contained only
two or three living-rooms. Placed together with
intervening cobble-stoned or red-bricked passages, they
faced the thoroughfares more or less as at present,
but especially along the turnpike. Within these
dwellings the greater part of the inhabitants huddled
themselves together like peas in pods. Smith's School
for very young children stood in the lane still bearing
its name, and near the Market-cross. The ancient
base, as placed there by Nicholas Criol in 1246, can
now be seen embedded in a semi-detached cottage wall.

Alluding to home life here in its saddest aspect the
poet says we

> . . . turn our view from dwellings simply neat
> To this infected row we term our street. . . .
> Between the roadway and the walls offence
> Invades all eyes and strikes on every sense;

[1] " Ancient Mansion."

There lie, obscene, at every open door
Heaps from the hearth and sweepings from the floor,
There hungry dogs from hungry children steal,
There pigs and chickens quarrel for a meal;
There dropsied infants wail without redress,
And all is want and woe and wretchedness.

.   .   .   .

Beds but ill parted by a paltry screen
Of paper'd lath or curtain dropt between;
Daughters and sons to yon compartments creep,
And parents here beside their children sleep.
Ye who have power, these thoughtless people part,
Nor let the ear be first to taint the heart.
Come !   Search within, nor sight nor smell regard;
The true physician walks the foulest ward,
See !   On the floor what frowsy patches rest !
What nauseous fragments on yon fractured chest !

.   .   .   .

To every house belongs a space of ground,
Of equal size, once fenced with paling round;
That paling now by slothful waste destroy'd,
Dead gorse and stumps of elder fill the void;
Here is no pavement, no inviting shop,
To give us shelter when compelled to stop;
But plashy puddles stand along the way
Fill'd by the rain of one tempestuous day,
And these so closely to the buildings run
That you must ford them for you cannot shun;
Though here and there convenient bricks are laid,
And door-side heaps afford their dubious aid.

But, even in the midst of these dark spots, upon so
favourable a landscape, as to bring home to us Bishop
Heber's well-known words, " Though every prospect
pleases, and only man is vile," we find such atoning
influences in operation as " The Amicable and Frugal
Society, founded on January 1st, 1771, for the benefit
of this parish and the circumjacent villages within
six computed miles thereof," an existing institution
with revised rules and another title, now supported by

National Insurance. The poet obviously has it in mind under " Social Meetings."

> The poor man has his Club; he comes and spends
> His hoarded pittance with his chosen friends;
> Nor this alone—a monthly dole he pays,
> To be assisted when his health decays;
> Some part his prudence, from the day's supply,
> For cares and troubles in his age lays by;
> The printed rules he guards with painted frame,
> And shows his children where to read his name.
> Those simple words his honest nature move,
> That bond of union tied by laws of love;
> This is his pride; it gives to his employ
> New value, to his home another joy;
> While a religious hope its balm applies
> For all his fate inflicts and all his State denies.

Indeed, the articles of agreement contain this significant allusion: " The members, for their mutual assistance and support, and to promote friendship, love, and benevolence, as far as they are able, hold themselves bound to each other in the faithful observance thereof."

Another society of doubtful origin and benefit except to those initiated into its mysteries and hieroglyphics, like those carved upon the church porch wall, is also referred to thus:

> Masons are ours, Freemasons—but, alas!
> To their own bards I leave the mystic class:
> In vain shall one, and not a gifted man,
> Attempt to sing of this enlightened clan:
> I know no Word, boast no directing Sign,
> And not one token of the race is mine.
> Yet if such blessings from their Order flow,
> We should be glad their moral code to know.

Then, again, in close connection this redeeming incident in " The School Cottager " :

> . . . ere she was born
> Her father died, her mother on that morn:
> The pious mistress of the School sustains
> Her parents' part, nor their affection feigns,
> But pitying feels:

After commenting upon the " fair scenes which give a peculiar charm to Croxton," as well as on others so disreputably bad, the poet next draws attention to its well-known house. The "Hall," as sometimes described, afforded interest in many ways at that time, and indeed right up to early Victorian days, when parties from Belvoir used to drive over to take tea there. A portion, rather ruinous in appearance, still remains, and distant views may be obtained from near the milestone on Ling's-hill. Close to this site also stood the Abbey where King John's viscera were buried. Here Crabbe says we

> . . . can but look, with many a sigh,
> On sacred buildings, doom'd in dust to lie;
> " On seats," they tell, " where priests mid tapers dim
> Breathed the warm prayer, or tuned the midnight hymn;
> Where trembling penitents their guilt confess'd,
> Where want and succour and contrition rest;
> There weary men from trouble found relief,
> There men in sorrow found repose from grief.
> To scenes like these the fainting soul retired;
> Revenge and anger in these cells expired;
> By pity soothed, remorse lost half her fears,
> And soften'd pride dropp'd penitential tears.
> Now all's lost, the earth where the Abbey stood
> Is layman's land, the glebe, the stream, the wood.

For at the dissolution Henry VIII. gave it to Thomas, first Earl of Rutland, whose successors built the mansion from the material during the early part of the eighteenth century. Several references are discovered in the *Works* under different titles and descriptions, which plainly point to the then hunting box and all the surroundings. For instance, on arrival,

>   . . . he went round and found
> Food for his wonder all the house around.
> There guns of various bore, and rods and lines,
> And all that man for deed of death designs
> In beast, or bird, or fish, or worm, or fly;
> Life in these last must means of death supply;
> The living bait is gorged, and both the victims die:
> Much had he seen, and everything he saw
> Excited pleasure not unmixed with awe.
> Leaving each room, he turn'd, as if once more
> To enjoy the pleasure that he felt before.
> " What then must their possessors feel ?　How grand
> And happy they who can such joys command ?
> For they may pleasures all their lives pursue,
> The winter pleasures and the summer's too—
> Pleasures for every hour in every day;
> Oh ! how their time must pass in joy away !

There is good reason for supposing that the chaplain had his first meal here. At all events, it must have been very early in the clerical career, because he appears so self-conscious of his humble birth and parentage. The father, we know, held a junior position in the Custom House, and sat in the quaint " Moot Hall " along with other borough bailiffs. The manner of reaching his destination, the kindly reception, together with some amusing reflections are graphically described in " The Patron ":

> Impatient by the morning mail conveyed,
> The happy guest his promised visit paid.
> And now arriving at the Hall, he tried
> For air composed, serene, and satisfied,
> As he had practised in his room alone,
> And there acquired a free and easy tone:
> There he had said, " Whatever the degree
> A man obtains, what more than man is he ?"
> And when arrived—" This room is but a room;
> Can ought we see the steady soul o'ercome ?
> Let me in all a manly firmness show,
> Upheld by talents, and their value know."

This reason urged; but it surpassed his skill
To be in act as manly as in will:
When he his Lordship and the Lady saw,
Brave as he was, he felt oppress'd with awe:
And spite of verse, that so much praise had won,
The poet found he was the Bailiff's son.

But dinner came, and the succeeding hours
Fix'd his weak nerves, and raised his failing powers . . .
Now was the Sister of his Patron seen—
A lovely creature, with majestic mien
Who, softly smiling, while she look'd so fair,
Praised the young poet with such friendly air.
Such winning frankness in her looks express'd,
And such attention to her brother's guest,
That so much beauty, join'd with speech so kind,
Raised strong emotions in the poet's mind,
Till reason fail'd his bosom to defend
From the sweet power of this enchanting friend.

Among the poet's greatest pleasures when residing
here, as well as at the Castle, was the freedom to
ramble about the private grounds of the estate at
different times during the year. He would then examine
its sylvan nature minutely, register any such striking
mental impressions as thus recorded:

These giant oaks by no man's order stand;
Heaven did the work, by no man was it plann'd.
Here I behold no puny works of art,
None give me reasons why these views impart,
Such charm to fill the mind, such to fill the heart.[1]

Some ascribe them to " Three Queens " and
" King Lud," whose names are found near the boundary
land of " Egypt." That story, however, is considered
legendary, although the entrenchments and plantations
are still recorded on the map, but not the " Salt Way."
The Saxons called the upland corner of Leicestershire bordering Lincoln, Nottingham, and Rutland,

[1] " Ancient Mansion."

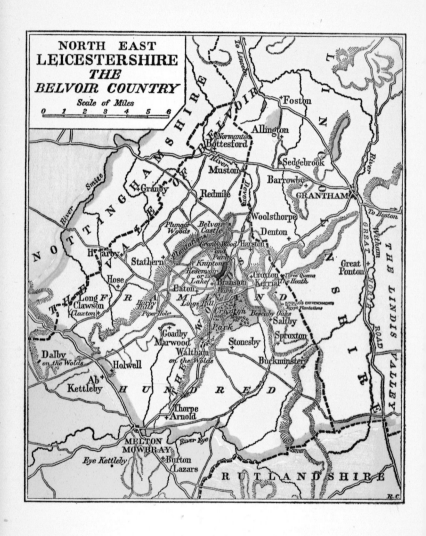

NORTH EAST
LEICESTERSHIRE
THE
BELVOIR COUNTRY

Scale of Miles

0 1 2 3 4 5 6

with Waltham village as the highest and centre point, roughly speaking, one wide expansive "Wold." They used this word for woody, lofty ground more open and cultivated than the wild forest. The oaks, therefore, like those of Bescaby and others, originated at the outskirts, in its north-easterly direction, and spread through the Lindis (Witham) Valley to the region beyond Buckminster. Thence they would expand westerly towards the foot of the hills near Harby and Plungar. Their extension from the south began at the River Eye about Thorpe Arnold and ended in the swampy marches of the Sedgebrook. After the Conquest, the Norman and Plantagenet Kings made these woods their happy hunting resorts. Then on April 26th, 1242, Henry II. gave the central portion to Bertram de Criol, Baron of Eye, from whose family the name Kerrial is derived. His successors, the Lords of the Manor, the Abbots of Croxton, and lastly the present owners, all contributed towards the making of this Park more or less as we know it, although now without the deer; and so the poet continues to describe from a site overlooking Branston:

How stately stand yon pines upon the hill,
How soft the murmurs of that living rill !
And o'er the Park's tall paling, scarcely higher,
Peeps the low Church and shows the modest spire.
Unnumber'd violets on those banks appear,
And all the first-born beauties of the year.
The grey-green blossoms of the willows bring
The large wild bees upon the labouring wing;
Then comes the summer, with augmented pride,
Whose pure small streams along the valleys glide:
Her richer Flora their brief charms display,
And, as the fruit advances, fall away.
Then shall th' autumnal yellow clothe the leaf,
What time the reaper binds the burden'd sheaf;
Then silent groves denote the dying year,
The morning frost and noontide gossamer;

Or here and there the gun whose loud report
Proclaims to man that Death is but his sport:
And then the wintry winds begin to blow,
Then fall the flaky stars of gathering snow,
When on the thorn, the ripening sloe, yet blue,
Takes the bright varnish of the morning dew;
The aged moss grows brittle on the pale,
The dry boughs splinter in the windy gale,
And every changing season of the year
Stamps on the scene its English character.
All so delightful, soothing, and serene !
Do you not feel it ?   Not enjoy the scene ?
Something it has which words will not express,
But rather hide, and make th' enjoyment less;
'Tis what our souls conceive, 'tis what our hearts confess.

Again, on another occasion shortly after marriage, when he was with his wife, we get pleasant peeps into their encounter by the fishpond stream with the Duke's chief agent, Mr. Thomas Thoroton, a wealthy connection of the Manners family. His son Robert acted as private secretary to the Lord-Lieutenant, then in Ireland. The chaplain and he, being about the same age and residing together at Belvoir, became great friends. Mr. and Mrs. Crabbe now receive a joyful communication from Dublin Castle:

Within the park, beside the bounding brook,
The social pair their usual ramble took:
And there the steward found them: they could trace
News in his look, and gladness in his face.
He was a man of riches, bluff and big,
With clean brown broadcloth, and with white cut wig;
He bore a cane of price, with riband tied,
And a fat spaniel waddled at his side.
To every being whom he met he gave
His looks expressive; civil, gay, or grave,
But condescending all; and each declared
How much he governed, and how well he fared.[1]

[1] " Tales of the Hall."

CHAPTER IX

CROXTON PARK AND CHEVELEY REMINISCENCES

He would have pictures, and of course a taste,
And found a thousand means his wealth to waste.
Newmarket steeds he bought at mighty cost;
They sometimes won, but nearly always lost.

To John Manners, the first ancestor of Crabbe's patron
to be raised to the Dukedom, belongs the distinction
of paving the way for the Belvoir Hunt, which originated with the hounds kennelled here. He would
sally forth from the Castle, make for the outbuildings
of the ruined Abbey, and having freed the buck-hounds,
start to hunt the deer on the " Wold," or in the " Vale "
beyond. From this stock crossed with others sprang
the present strain. Later the poet in his *Natural
History* says: " Many foxes were found here, and two
beautiful ones of the black kind were turned off from
Croxton Park by the Duke of Rutland." It appears
that this nobleman built the hunting-box and also
made " the addition of the picture room " at the
Castle. He first began to hunt the fox, a pleasure to
which he and " his more distinguished son the Marquis
of Granby were devoted, in 1727." The recently
deceased grandson evidently derived his generous disposition, artistic and scholastic talents, as well as a
" taste " for racing, from these forbears. The biographer now explains the situation during his father's
stay here. " The establishment of race horses (at
Cheveley), hunters and hounds were extensive because
it was held to be part of a nobleman's duty that they
should be so, but these things were rather for the enjoyment of his friends than for his own. He was suffi-

ciently interested to join in them occasionally, but he would frequently dismiss a splendid party from his gates, and himself ride accompanied only by Mr. Crabbe to converse on literary topics." Mr. Thomas Thoroton with " much " else also " governed " the Hunt, not only during the Viceroyalty, but for several years afterwards to 1791. His son Robert had the reputation for being the most intrepid rider of that decade, and often amused his friend in this and other respects. The chaplain, too, could ride, though he had never been known to be well mounted. This is admitted in a reference to " Gerard Abblett," a farmer proud,

> Who trots to market on a steed so fine,
> That when I meet him, I'm ashamed of mine.

And so far as concerned actual participation in the sport he did not figure at all except when attending a meet near at hand, so probably that afforded an opportunity to " tease " him. For, judging from certain reflections in the poem published about this time, he viewed fox-hunting for the clergy in the usual official light, illustrated as follows:

> Say ye, oppress'd by some fantastic woes,
> Some jarring nerve that baffles your repose;
> Who press the downy couch, while slaves advance
> With timid eye, to read the distant glance;
> Who with sad prayers the weary doctor tease,
> To name the nameless ever-new disease;
> Who with mock patience dire complaints endure,
> Which real pain and that alone can cure;
> How would ye bear in real pain to lie,
> Despised, neglected, left alone to die ?
> But ere his death some pious doubts arise,
> Some simple fears, which " bold bad " men despise;
> Fain would he ask the parish-priest to prove
> His title certain to the joys above:

For this he sends the murmuring nurse, who calls
The holy stranger to these dismal walls:
And doth not he, the pious man, appear,
He, " passing rich with forty pounds a year ?"
Ah ! no; a shepherd of a different stock,
And far unlike him, feeds this little flock:
A jovial youth, who thinks his Sunday's task
As much as God or man can fairly ask;
The rest he gives to loves and labours light,
To fields the morning, and to feasts the night;
None better skill'd the noisy pack to guide,
To urge their chase, to cheer them or to chide;
A sportsman keen, he shoots through half the day,
And, skill'd at whist, devotes the night to play:
Then, while such honours bloom around his head,
Shall he sit sadly by the sick man's bed,
To raise the hope he feels not, or with zeal
To combat fears that e'en the pious feel ?[1]

These couplets, however, were composed almost on
arrival from town, or in any case before the poet could
possibly gain a true perspective of rural life in this
neighbourhood, which even then had acquired considerable reputation for fox-hunting. As the author of
Highways and Byways in Leicestershire justly maintains,
public opinion is still charitable towards sporting
parsons, and there is no disposition to think the worse
of a rector who can ride to hounds or bring down his
bird. The tradition is old and strong in the county.
Besides we are told he afterwards made attempts in
one direction, if not both.

Crabbe took immense delight in telling stories.
Indeed, his poetical works as a whole are devoted to
tales more than any other subject in particular. Many
refer to persons whom he had met and known, usually
very well. A few concern himself, either directly or
indirectly, but never quite autobiographically. Thus,
in the first of the " Posthumous " series, the son in-

---

[1] " The Village."

forms us that his father's executors " think it right to preserve certain verses in a note, as they appear to leave little doubt that the story was in fact suggested by the poet's recollection of his own boyish visits, when an apothecary's apprentice, to Cheveley, a seat of the noble family with whom, in after years, he lived as Chaplain." There can be no question as to the propriety. Indeed, some minor details in the longer portion from which the accompanying adaptation has been taken—Peter and his pony, for instance —are undoubtedly reminiscent of a Christmas-tide ride from Wickhambrook in 1768. But, obviously, the more important circumstances could not have been recorded until nearly twenty years later, during the period under consideration. For then only had the Rev. G. Crabbe the opportunity of seeing certain pictures at the Castle. Let us consider one, " The Nativity," painted by the great artist Reynolds in 1780, exhibited at the Royal Academy, and purchased by the Duke of Rutland for 1,200 guineas. Beechy, in his *Memoir*, says: " This fine work of art was, unfortunately, destroyed by fire at Belvoir Castle." The dimensions of the large canvas were 12 by 18 feet, a considerable height, and the composition consisted in wonderfully grouping thirteen figures—the Virgin Mary, Joseph and the Angels, with the Infant Christ in the centre. This painting, originally designed for New College, Oxford, may have been intended for the private chapel at Belvoir, much in the same way as the present altar-piece by Murillo. In that case, the chaplain would, naturally, gain his impressions whilst officiating in the actual building. So we may presume to think that those portions of the tale concerning the Castle were composed either on the spot, or, what seems more likely, at Croxton Park House before marriage, when he had more time to reflect, and where other circumstances so aptly apply. Then, not wishing to identify himself and patron, he conceals the plot, and even leaves instructions that " Silford Hall " shall not be published until after his death.

THE STORY

(told in dialogue between young Master Crabbe and an elderly lady friend):

> Then to the Chapel moved the friendly pair,
> And well for Peter that his guide was there !
> Dim, silent, solemn was the scene—he felt
> The cedar's power, that so unearthly smelt;
> And then the stain'd, dark, narrow windows threw
> Strange partial beams on pulpit, desk and pew.
> Upon the Altar glorious to behold
> Stood a vast pair of candlesticks in gold,
> With candles tall, and large, and firm, and white,
> Such as the halls of giant kings would light.
> There was an organ, too, but now unseen;
> A long black curtain served it for a screen.
> Not so the clock, that, both by night and day,
> Click'd the short moments as they pass'd away.
> " Is this a Church, and does the parson read "—
> Said Peter—" here ?   I mean a Church indeed."
> " Indeed, it is, or as a Church is used,"
> Was the reply, and Peter deeply mused,
> Not without awe.   His sadness to dispel,
> They sought the gallery, and then all was well.
> Yet enter'd there, although so clear his mind
> From every fear substantial and defined,
> Yet there remain'd some touch of native fear,
> Of something awful to the eye and ear,
> A ghostly voice might sound—a ghost itself appear.
> On a tall picture, Peter gazed and stood
> In admiration—" 'twas so dearly good !"
> " For how much money, think you, then, my lad,
> Is such a ' dear good picture ' to be had ?"
> " I tell the price," quoth Peter, " I as soon
> Could tell the price of pictures in the moon. . . ."
> " 'Tis by Sir Joshua.   Did you ever see
> A Babe so charming ?"   " No, indeed," said he:

" I wonder how he could that look invent,
That seems so shy, and yet so innocent !"
" Why look so earnest, Boy ?"   " Because it brings
To me a story of some awful things."
" Tell then thy story."   He, who never stay'd
For words or matter, instantly obey'd.
" A holy pilgrim to a city sail'd,
Where every sin o'er sinful men prevail'd,
Who, when he landed, look'd in every street,
As he was wont, a busy crowd to meet."
Just at this time, when Peter's heart began
To admit the fear that shames the valiant man,
He paused—but why.   " Here's one my guard to be;
When thus protected, none can trouble me."
Then rising look'd he round and lo ! alone was he,
Three ponderous doors with locks of shining brass
Seem'd to invite the trembling boy to pass;
But fear forbade, till fear itself supplied
The place of courage, and at length he tried.
He grasp'd the key—alas ! though great his need,
The key turn'd not, the bolt would not recede.
Try then again; for what will not distress ?
Again he tried, and with the same success.
Yet one remains, remains untried one door—
A failing hope, for two had fail'd before;
But a bold Prince, with fifty doors in sight,
Tried forty-nine before he found the right—
Before he mounted on the brazen horse,
And o'er the walls pursued his airy course.
So his cold hand on this last key he laid:
" Now turn," said he; the treacherous bolt obey'd—
The door receded—bringing full in view
The dim, dull chapel, pulpit, desk, and pew.
Deeply he sigh'd, nor from his heart could chase
The dread of dying in that dismal place;
Anger and sorrow in his bosom strove,
And banish'd all that yet remained of love;
When soon despair had seized the trembling boy—
But hark ! a voice ! the sound of peace and joy.
" Where art thou, lad ?"   " Oh ! here am I in doubt,
And sorely frightened—can you let me out ?"
" Oh, yes, my child; it was indeed a sin,

Forgetful as I was, to bolt you in.
I left you reading, and from habit lock'd
The door behind me, but in truth am shock'd
To serve you thus; but we will make amends
For such mistake. Come, cheerly, we are friends."
" Oh, yes !" said Peter, quite alive to be
So kindly used, and have so much to see,
And having so much seen; his way he spied,
Forgot his peril and rejoin'd his guide.

  . . . .

" Now haste to dinner;"—
He went and sat with equal shame, and pride,
A welcome guest at Madam Johnson's side.
At his right hand was Mistress Kitty placed,
And Lucy, maiden sly, the stripling faced.
Then each the proper seat at table took—
Groom, butler, footman, laundress, coachman, cook;
For all their station and their office knew,
Nor sat as rustics or the rabble do.
With much respect each other they address'd
And all encouraged their enchanted guest.
Wine, fruit, and sweetmeats closed repast so long,
And Mistress Flora sang an opera song.
Such was the day the happy boy had spent,
And forth delighted from the Hall he went;
Bowing his thanks, he mounted on his steed,
More largely fed than he was wont to feed;
And well for Peter that his pony knew
From whence he came, the road he should pursue;
For the young rider had his mind estranged
From all around, disturb'd, and disarranged,
In pleasing tumult, in a dream of bliss,
Enjoy'd but seldom in a world like this

CHAPTER X

HOME AND VILLAGE LIFE AT STATHERN

This, this is beauty; cast, I pray, your eyes
On this my glory ! see the grace ! the size !
Was ever stem so tall, so stout, so strong,
Exact in breadth, in just proportion long ?
These brilliant hues are all distinct and clean,
No kindred tint, no blending streaks between:
This is no shaded, run off, pin-eyed thing:
A king of flowers, a flower for England's King.

THE poet, botanist, and naturalist has given us many
instances of his keen interest in all the country's varied
beauty while walking, or rather rambling, with
his young wife over hill and valley, and especially
amongst the trees and woods on the estate, like the last
visit to Croxton Park. But, towards the end of the
period under consideration, home cares and parochial
duties claimed no unimportant share of his time and
attention. Indeed, from now onwards for a few years
we shall be more likely to find the parental Crabbe
in the nurseries, either amongst the children or the
flowers. Having, then, returned from a journey we
may say:

There is my friend, the Father; strong desires
Reign in his breast; 'tis beauty he admires;
See ! to the shady grove he wings his way,
And feels in hope the raptures of the day—
Eager he looks, and soon, to glad his eyes,
From the sweet bower, by nature form'd, arise
Bright troops of virgin moths and fresh-born butterflies;
Who woke that morning from their half-year's sleep,
To fly o'er flowers where they were wont to creep—

STATHERN CHURCH AND RECTORY.

Heawood (Melton Mowbray)

facing p. 73.

Above the sovereign oak, a sovereign skims,
The purple Emp'ror, strong in wing and limbs;
There fair Camilla takes her flight serene,
Adonis-blue, and Paphia-silver queen;
With every filmy fly from mead or bower,
And hungry Sphinx: who threads the honey'd flower;
She o'er the larkspur's bed, where sweets abound,
Views ev'ry bell, and hums th' approving sound;
Poised on her busy plumes with feeling nice
She draws from every flower, nor tries a floret twice.

Stathern seems always to have had a rather un-
enviable reputation for poaching. Anyhow, there were
frequent troubles with the Duke's keepers, so the
parson, in playful satire, refers to personal freedom
from suspicion in his own tiny preserve:

He fears no bailiff's wrath, no Baron's blame,
His is untax'd and undisputed game;
Nor less the place of curious plant he knows,
He both his flora and his fauna shows.

Then, should we be privileged, as some say, to step
back into those " good old days of long ago," open our
eyes and peep into the Rectory, having a culinary
garden on one side, and a pleasant lawn with her-
baceous borders and a copse on the other, this pretty
pen-picture in vivid prose by the biographer would
doubtless be seen:

How delightful is it to recall the innocent
feelings of unbounded love, confidence, and respect
associated with the earliest visions of my parents.
My father entered into all our pleasures, and
soothed and cheered us in all our little griefs with
such overflowing tenderness that it was no wonder
we almost worshipped him. My first recollection
is of his carrying me up to his private room to
prayers, in the summer evenings, about sunset,
and rewarding my silence and attention afterwards

with a view of the flower garden through his prism. But, I think, even earlier than these are my first recollections of my mother . . . combing my hair one evening by the light of the fire which hardly broke the long shadows of the room and singing the plaintive air of " Kitty Fell," till, though I could not have been more than three years old, the melody found its way into my heart, and the tears dropped down so profusely that I was glad the darkness concealed them. How mysterious is shame without guilt !

And then when both father and mother were able to go outside, we should find how

Pleasant it was to see them in their walk
Round their small garden, and to hear them talk;
Three are their children, and their love refrains
From all offence—none murmurs, none complains;
Whether a toy amused them, speech, or play,
Their looks were lively, and their hearts were gay;
There no forced efforts for delight were made,
Joy came with prudence, and without parade;
Their common comforts they had all in view,
Light were their troubles and their wishes few,
Thrift made them easy for the coming day,
Religion took the dread of death away;
A cheerful spirit still ensured content,
And love smiled round them wheresoe'er they went.

Undoubtedly Crabbe dearly loved this garden where, for the first time, he who had been so fond of herbs and flowers possessed a place to plant and inspect them. Indeed, if at home on a summer's evening father could not be found in the study or the nursery, mother would have no such difficulty on looking outside, for there she could almost certainly see him, either busily mowing the lawn or else sitting on the rustic bench admiring the multi-coloured beds and hearkening to the pleasant sounds around.

And where is he ?   Ah ! doubtless in those scenes
Of his best days, amid the vivid greens,
Fresh with unnumber'd rills, where ev'ry gale
Breathes the rich fragrance of the neighb'ring vale.
Smiles not his wife, and listens as there comes
The night-bird's music from the thick'ning glooms ?
And as he sits with all these treasures nigh,
Blaze not with fairy-light the phosphor-fly,
When like a sparkling gem it wheels illumined by ?
This is the joy that now so plainly speaks
In the warm transient flushing of his cheeks;
For he is listening to the fancied noise
Of his own children, eager in their joys.[1]

The very fact that the poet had a fondness for this plot and the little spinney skirting the drive from the road helped to create an exaggerated impression of disagreeableness, because on arrival the rector had just cause to grumble about the way his neighbours spoilt the shrubs and broke down the hedges in their eagerness to gather kindling. Quite naturally steps were taken to prevent them. Accordingly he wrote to the Duke, then in Ireland, to complain about the " petty larcenies " of his poor parishioners, and added the hope that " as his Grace's wood was so convenient for them, they will not be so wicked as to steal from their pastor what his patron can so amply supply."[2]

If ever fretful thought disturb'd his breast,
If aught of gloom that cheerful mind oppress'd,
It sprang from innovation; it was then
He spake of mischief made by restless men.

However, as a rule we may more correctly affirm and say:

Our priest was cheerful and in season gay
His frequent visits seldom fail'd to please.
Easy himself, he sought his neighbours' ease;

[1] " The Parting Hour."
[2] Historical MSS. Commission.

To the small garden with delight he came
And gave successive flowers a summer's fame;
These he presented, with a grace his own,
To his fair friends, and made their beauties known,
Not without moral compliment, how they
" Like flowers were sweet, and must like flowers decay."

The poet was assisted often by an equally enthusiastic, though loquacious and pedantic, gardener so
called, like most parsons' men, whose special job was
to look after the vegetables, the one-horse chaise, and
to make himself generally useful. But he liked, on all
possible occasions, to find any excuse except the right
one for being with his master on the other side of the
house so as to listen to his talk. Then would come
opportunities for enlightenment by giving him botanical
explanations:

But I digress, and lo ! an infant train
Appear, and call me to my task again.
" Why Lonicera wilt thou name thy child ?"
I asked the gardener's wife in accents mild.
" We have a right," replied the sturdy dame;
And Lonicera was the infant's name.
If next a son shall yield our gardener joy,
Then Hyacinthus shall be that fair boy;
And if a girl, they will at length agree
That Belladonna that fair maid shall be.

Then later on:

Not Darwin's self had more delight to sing
Of floral courtship in the awaken'd spring,
Than Peter Pratt, who, simpering, loves to tell
How rise the stamens, as the pistils swell;
How bend and curl the moist-top to the spouse,
And give and take the vegetable vows;
How those esteem'd of old, but tips and chives,
Are tender husbands and obedient wives;
Who live and love within the sacred bower,
That bridal bed, the vulgar term a flower.

Now the biographer, referring to his father's curacy-in-charge, says: "The situation prevented him from being drawn into any sort of unpleasant disputes with the villagers." Such a statement, then, leads to enquiry, which shows that the glebe and certain meadows in the parish were under common right distraint !

The Archdeacon of Stamford, as rector, with 365 acres, and two Lords of the Manors, with fully 1,600, were at variance over the land question.

> But think, ye rectors and ye curates, think,
> Who are your friends, and at their frailties wink;
> Conceive not—mounted on your Sunday-throne,
> Your firebrands fall upon your foes alone;
> They strike your patrons—and should all withdraw,
> In whom your wisdoms may discern a flaw
> You would the flower of all your audience lose,
> And spend your crackers on their empty pews.

We are told the Reignes's family had a considerable interest in it very anciently.[1]

Then, in 1541, the possessions belonging to Croxton Abbey and Belvoir Priory derived through Margaret de Rosse were granted by Henry VIII. to Thomas, Earl of Rutland. Meanwhile, it is said that Sir Thomas de Reynes's estate, including a moiety of the manor, with the advowson of the church, passed, through purchase, in 1487, to the Master and Fellows of St. Peter's College, Cambridge. Members of this family, however, continued in residence until nearly the middle of the seventeenth century. Their descendants, then, were the parochial Esquires. But whether they occupied the remodelled granary buildings belonging to the religious houses named above, bordering Hose or Eaton, is not disclosed. The poet, knowing the circumstances, and not wishing to identify himself or anyone else personally in those

---

[1] Lords of Clifton and Okeley; from the Chetwynd MS.

troubles, nevertheless affords us an insight into both sides of the question as decided by the Enclosure Acts under Elizabeth and George III.:

> " Alas !   Alas !"   Old England now may say,
> " My glory withers; it has had its day;
> We're fallen on evil times; men read and think;
> Our bold forefathers loved to fight and drink.
> Then lived the good Squire Asgill—what a change
> Has death and fashion shown us at the Grange !
> He bravely thought it best became his rank
> That all his tenants and his tradesmen drank,
> Praising aloud the liquor and the host
> And striving who should venerate him most !
> No pride had he, and there was difference small
> Between the master's and the servants' hall.
> And here or there the guests were welcome all,
> Of Heaven's free gifts—he took no special care,
> He never quarrel'd for a simple hare,
> But sought, by giving sport, a sportsman's name.
> Himself a poacher, though at other game;
> He never planted nor enclosed—his trees
> Grew like himself, untroubled and at ease;
> Bounds of all kinds he hated, and had felt
> Chok'd and imprison'd in a modern belt,
> Which some rare genius now has twined about
> The good old house, to keep old neighbours out."

These territorial changes from open to enclosed spaces, exceedingly complicated in nature, were not, it is true, altogether good. But, on the other hand, like all revolutions, they were far from bad, though unpopular at first, for the ultimate results were land economy, better farming, larger crops, and increased incomes.[1] At the end of the decade (1790) we find from a Royal Commission report that there were in the parish 2,000 acres open fields, moderate land, with a few small enclosures, and producing wheat, beans, and barley. It also possessed " con-

[1] See H. Rider Haggard in *Rural England*, 1906.

siderable common pastures and many gardens belonging to the poorer dwellings." And then it sums up:
" But, notwithstanding these apparent and, we should
suppose, real advantages, the poor at Stathern are no
objects of envy to the poorest in the surrounding
villages." Parliament ratified the recommendations
two years later, and the passing of the old régime is
thus illustrated:

> The father dead, the son has found a wife,
> And lives a formal, proud, unsocial life;
> The lands are now enclosed; the tenants all,
> Save at a rent-day, never see the hall;
> Oh ! could the ghost of our good Squire arise,
> And see such change; would it believe its eyes ?
> Would it not glide about from place to place,
> And mourn the manners of a feebler race ?
>
> At that long table where the servants found
> Mirth and abundance while the year went round;
> Where not a measure in the room was kept,
> And but one rule—they tippled till they slept—
> Then would it flit to higher rooms, and stay
> To view a dull, dress'd company at play;
> All the old comfort, all the genial fare
> For ever gone ! How sternly would it stare;
> And though it might not to their view appear,
> 'Twould cause among them lassitude and fear;
> Then wait to see—where he delight has seen—
> The dire effect of fretfulness and spleen.
> Such were the worthies of these better days;
> We had their blessings—they shall have our praise.[1]

Then one or two passages in the same poem specially
mark the author's characteristic compassion towards
the poor, aged sufferers, who, unable to adjust their
lives to the altered conditions imposed by these Acts,
were obliged to leave the village. That he is thinking
about instances which came under his observation

[1] Ben Bow in " The Borough."

during residence here is fairly obvious from the choice of illustrations found in the following lines:

> I own it grieves me to behold them sent
> From their old home; 'tis pain, 'tis punishment,
> To leave each scene familiar, every face,
> For a new people and a stranger race.
> The grateful hunter, when his horse is old,
> Wills not the useless favourite to be sold;
> He knows his former worth, and gives him place
> In some fair pasture, till he runs his race.

And, as the heart expands in sympathy, he enquires whether the labourer has done less worthy service than this discarded but well-provided hack, so contentedly grazing in the meadow.

> Shall we not then contribute to their ease,
> In their old haunts, where ancient objects please ?
> That, till their sight shall fail them, they may trace
> The well-known prospect and the long-loved face,
> The noble oak, in distant ages seen,
> With far-stretch'd boughs and foliage fresh and green,
> Though now its bare and forky branches show
> How much it lacks the vital warmth below,
> The stately ruin yet our wonder gains,
> Nay, moves our pity, without thought of pains.
> Much more shall real wants and cares of age
> Our gentler passions in their cause engage;
> Drooping and burthen'd with a weight of years,
> What venerable ruin man appears !
> How worthy pity, love, respect, and grief
> He claims protection—he compels relief—
> And shall we send him from our view, to brave
> The storms abroad, when we at home might save,
> And let a stranger dig our ancient brother's grave ?
> No ! We will shield him from the storm he fears,
> And when he falls, embalm him with our tears.

Again, amongst certain rare lyrical stanzas, preserved and long afterwards tacked on to a posthumous tale called " Farewell and Return," we are reminded

of these bygone changes. The poet is supposed to be
rambling in the locality when—

> A man approach'd me, by his grandchild led—
> A blind old man, and she a fair young maid,
> Listening in love to what her grandsire said.
> And thus, with gentle voice, he spoke:
> " Come, lead me, lassie, to the shade,
> Where willows grow beside the brook,
> For well I know the sound it made."
>
> The lass replied: " The trees are fled;
> They've cut the brook a straighter bed;
> No shades the present lords allow,
> The miller only murmurs how
> The waters now his mill forsake,
> And form a pond they call a lake."

The allusion points eastwards to the Grange's water-
mill at Eaton, and the construction, or enlargement, of
the present Knipton Reservoir. Indeed, the long,
low-lying ravine beginning very near the Stathern
hills and stretching outwards, through Branston to
Woolsthorpe, became a favourite haunt for herbs and
flowers, as already recorded. But, once more, to
change the direction:

> " Lassie, lead me to the west,
> Where grow the elm-trees thick and tall,
> Where rooks unnumber'd build their nest,
> Deliberate birds and prudent all;
> Their notes, indeed, are harsh and rude,
> But they're a social multitude."
>
> " The rooks are shot, the trees are fell'd,
> The nest and nursery all expell'd . . .
> The Churchway walk is now no more,
> And men must other ways explore;
> Though this, indeed, promotion gains,
> For this, the park's new wall contains;
> And here, I fear, we shall not meet
> A shade—although, perchance, a seat."

7

The crows may have left their haunts for a while, but they have returned to the Stathern and Plungar Woods, as everybody in the neighbourhood knows. Besides, on the brow of the hill at the end of Combs Plantation is a rustic bench in much the same position as of yore, with overhanging branches, once again affording full protection from the setting sun. But then, disappointed, tired, and thirsty:

> " My lassie, lead the way
> To Comfort's Home, the ancient inn,
> That something holds, if we can pay—
> Old David is our living kin;
> A servant once, he still preserves
> His name, and in his office serves."
> " Alas !   That mine should be the fate
> Old David's sorrows to relate,
> But they were brief; not long before
> He died, his office was no more.
> The kennel stands upon the ground,
> With something of the former sound."
> " O, then," the grieving man replied,
> " No further, lassie, let me stray;
> Here's nothing left of ancient pride,
> Of what was grand, of what was gay;
> But all is changed, is lost, is sold—
> All, all that's left is chilling cold.
> I seek for comfort here in vain,
> Then lead me to my cot again."

CHAPTER XI

AB-KETTLEBY AND HOLWELL: WEIRD AND QUACK STORIES

Care lives with all; no rules, no precepts save
The wise from wo, no fortitude the brave;
Grief is to man as certain as the grave:
Tempests and storms in life's whole progress rise,
And hope shines dimly through o'erclouded skies;
Some drops of comfort on the favour'd fall,
But showers of sorrow are the lot of all.[1]

FROM other portions of this period's poetry may be found certain indications as to interesting local and historical estates. One used to belong to Sir John Digby of Kettleby—third son of that renowned Everard Digby, high sheriff of the County of Rutland, who fell at the battle of Towton in 1440, under the banner of the unfortunate Henry VI.—as his descendants had lands, possessions, and advowsons in the immediate vicinity. For instance, one Sir John was patron of the Claxon living (Long Clawson), 1508; again, in the seventeenth century we find at Ab*b* Kettleby Church, amongst crumbling monumental remains, the elegantly designed mural tomb with (formerly at the bottom) kneeling figure of another Everard, a baronet, who died at Holiwell, and was buried 1628. He was the last member of the ancient house of Tilton to reside here at Eye Hall. The widow belonged to the neighbouring Sacheveralls, of Burton Lazars, as the arms, a fleur-de-lis impaling five *Bouts* or *Bougets* of water surmounted by the ostrich crest, signify.

The chaplain knew that Charles II. had stayed here

---

[1] " The Library."

for breakfast with his retinue before going on to the
Castle; and about the close intimacy existing between
the two families of the Royal cause; so he would not
unnaturally desire to explore the Vale's extreme south-
west corner in order to see the place.

Thus, in the tenth tale of " Farewell and Return "
there are the following lines with regard to its former
status, as he imagined, early in the previous century:

> There with its tenantry about reside
> A genuine English race, the country's pride;
> And now a Lady, last of all that race
> Is the departing spirit of the place.
> Hers is the last of all that noble blood
> That flow'd through generations brave and good;
> And if there dwells a native pride in her,
> It is the pride of name and character. . . .
> Still are her habits of the ancient kind,
> She knows the poor, the sick, the lame, the blind;
> She holds, so she believes, her wealth in trust,
> And being kind with her is being just.
> Though soul and body she delights to aid,
> Yet of her skill she's prudently afraid;
> So to her Chaplain's care she this commends,
> And when that craves, the village Doctor sends.
> At Church attendance she requires of all
> Who would be held in credit at the Hall;
> A due respect to each degree she shows,
> And pays the debt that every mortal owes;
> 'Tis by opinion that respect is led,
> The rich esteem because the poor are fed.

This old estate, containing a fine Tudor mellow and
rustic-like residence, then passed, by purchase, into the
ownership of a *nouveau riche* named Hackett, the spendthrift, who soon began to hack down the timber,
to demolish the venerable buildings, and to perpetrate
other acts of wanton vandalism in order to bring it
up to date.   At least, this is the idea in the poet's mind,
based upon some local tradition.   We now, like Rip

Van Winkle, allow about twenty years interval before
the scene is revisited, when, after staying the night at
Melton Mowbray, he portrays its present aspect:

> I leave the town, and take a well-known way,
> To that old mansion in the closing day,
> When beams of golden light are shed around,
> And sweet is every sight and every sound,
> Pass but this hill, and I shall then behold
> The seat so honour'd, so admired of old—
>
> Alas, I see a change,
> Of odious kind, and lamentably strange.
> Who had done this ?   The good old Lady lies
> Within her tomb; but who could this advise ?
> What barbarous hand could all this mischief do,
> And spoil a noble house to make it new ?
> Who had done this ?   Some genuine son of Trade
> Has all this dreadful devastation made;
> Some man with line and rule, and evil eye,
> Who could no beauty in a tree descry,
> Some true admirer of the time's reform,
> Who strips an ancient dwelling like a storm,
> Strips it of all its dignity and grace
> To put his own dear fancies in their place. . . .
> The things themselves are pleasant to behold
> But not like those which we beheld of old—
> That half-hid mansion with its wide domain,
> Unbound and unsubdued—but sighs are vain;
> It is the rage of Taste—the rule and compass reign.

How fresh, realistic and eventful this description !
It happened more than 250 years ago ! History,
indeed, has a wonderful way in repeating itself ! Have
not similar instances occurred under our own eyes all
over England since the war ? Who could surpass
Crabbe in this kind of domestic verse for force, truth,
and pathos, despite his faults ? We enquire because
some—see Firth's *Highways and Byways in Leicestershire*—
give him less credit than his due, and even wrongly
ascribe to Cowper lines taken from " The Borough "

with reference to the Digby monuments and those belonging to their connections, Skeffington of Skeffington. Still we are much indebted to the author for the following weird story about Hackett's death, as an illustration: " On November 25th, 1686, he was dining with Mr. Bennett, at Welby, in the company of the Earl of Rutland and other gentlemen. A storm threatened, and Hackett went three times to the front door to look at the sky. The third time he did so an owl flew in and perched on his shoulder. Returning to the dining-room, he told the company of the incident, and the superstitious held that such an omen boded dire misfortune. Hackett laughed at their fears. It would take more than an owl to frighten him. When he rose to go, and his host offered to send a groom to see him safe home, he refused. But Bennett was so nervous that he privily told the groom not to let Hackett out of his sight. Hackett then set off, but after going a little way he observed the groom following him, angrily sent him back to his master, and then went on alone. The next morning, a shepherd found him lying helpless in the road, and he never spoke again. Such was the end of the last of the Hacketts, after he had dissipated a splendid fortune. From his senseless fury in attacking the groom I infer that he was none too sober, and that he was thrown heavily from his horse." Of their memorial Crabbe says:

> Our sons shall see its more degraded state,
> The tomb of grandeur hastens to its fate;
> That marble arch, our sexton's favourite show,
> With all those ruff'd and painted pairs below;
> The noble Lady and the Lord who rest
> Supine, as courtly dame and warrior drest,
> All are departed from their state sublime,
> Mangled and wounded in their war with time,
> Colleagued with mischief; here a leg is fled
> And lo ! the Baron with but half a head:
> Midway is cleft the arch; the very base
> Is battered round and shifted from its place.

The allusion to Holiwell, so spelt on ancient records in the chapelry and hamlet of Abb, or Ab-Kettleby (the hyphen connection is an abbreviation for Abbot, the head of the religious house to which it belonged), might easily have led the poet to enquire into this origin, and at the same time into the sacred epithet applied to its well. To begin with the latter, Nichols (alluding to the source of the Smite, a tributary to the river Trent) calls it a famous chalybeate spring or spa, formerly more reputable, which is considered as serviceable in many distempers, whence it obtained the name of Holiwell. And from his account there is sufficient evidence to prove that at least one parishioner, a farmer, believed in the efficacy of the slightly disagreeable liquor, seeing he left an annuity to repair the site and surroundings as a mark and thank-offering for his cure. But even so that would hardly justify its claim to sanctity. The reason, then, may be discovered from the ecclesiastical history of the place, because it is definitely affirmed that the chapelry of Holywell paid a yearly rent to the preceptory at Dalby-on-the-Wolds. So perhaps the Knights Templars had been able to confirm the tradition concerning a certain pious person, among a few ladies, who in the early days of Christianity suffered persecution at or near some watering site, and in consequence added a halo to its reputation. But others have differed as to whether the sacred spring or river happened to be in Mercia or East Anglia, with an interval of 270 years. So what did Crabbe, the cute investigator, suppose? His personal conviction is indicated by choosing from the Calendar of Canonised Virgins and other honourable women a name for the suggestive impersonation of quackery, and in this instance by refraining from any satirical comment which might sound irreverent. He does, however, permit two former acquaintances to give us a clue to its probable title, for our old blind friend mutters—

Well I know the sound it made,
When dashing o'er the stony rill,
It murmur'd to St. Osyth's Mill. . . .
    Then, lassie, lead thy grandsire on,
And so the holy water bring;
A cup is fastened to the stone,
And I would taste the healing spring
That soon its rocky cist forsakes
And green its mossy passage makes.

This saint is said to have fallen into the river when crossing a bridge, and to have been providentially rescued from drowning, after being in the water for three days, by the Abbess Modwenna, from Burton-on-Trent Nunnery. Leland, usually a reliable authority, puts the event down at A.D. 600. Butler, of equal credit, is dubious regarding this event occurring there or in Essex, where the little town near Clacton-on-Sea is the only place still named in her honour. He says the virgin was martyred on October 7th, 870, the great year of the Danish invasion, near here in the Midlands, and on the spot where she suffered there sprang up a fountain having miraculous virtues. Osyth, in fact, is only a name imposed on that place or a similar one at Ab-Kettleby to create a fictitious sanctity. Truly, then, may the niece, with her clear vision, assure us:

The holy spring is turned aside,
The rock is gone, the stream is dried;
The plough has levelled all around,
And here is now no holy ground.

Yes, Holwell has long ago dropped the missing vowel, for, as its up-to-date historian amusingly infers, " No one takes much heed of local chalybeate springs in these days of cash chemists." Now the poet, who could speak from chemical and medical experience, tells us a good story on quackery in the so-called medical profession:

Ere for the world's I left the cares of School,
One I remember who assumed the fool;
A part well suited—when the idler boys
Would shout around him and he loved the noise;
They called him " Neddy "; Neddy had the art
To play with skill his ignominious part;
When he his trifles would for sale display,
And act the mimic for a Schoolboy's pay.
For many years he plied his humble trade,
And used his tricks and talents to persuade;
The fellow barely read, but chanced to look
Among the fragments of a tatter'd book;
Where after many efforts made to spell
One puzzling word, he found it oxymel;
A potent thing, 'twas said to cure the ills
Of ailing lungs—the oxymel of squills;
Squills he procured, but found the bitter strong
And most unpleasant; none would take it long;
But the pure acid and the sweet would make
A med'cine numbers would for pleasure take.
There was a fellow near, an artful knave,
Who knew the plan, and much assistance gave;
He wrote the puffs, and every talent plied
To make it sell; it sold, and then he died.
Now all the profit fell to Ned's control,
And Pride and Avarice quarrel'd for his soul;
When mighty profits by the trash were made,
Pride built a palace; Avarice groan'd and paid;
Pride placed the signs of grandeur all about
And Avarice barr'd his friends and children out.
Now see him, Doctor ! yes, the idle fool,
The butt, the robber of the lads at School,
Who then knew nothing, nothing since acquired;
Became a Doctor, honoured and admired.
His dress, his frown, his dignity were such,
Some who had known him thought his knowledge much;
Nay, men of skill, of apprehension quick,
Spite of their knowledge, trusted him when sick;
Though he could neither reason, write, nor spell,
They yet had hope his trash would make them well;
And while they scorn'd his parts they took his oxymel. . . .
Hence impositions of the grossest kind,

> Hence thought is feeble, understanding blind;
> Hence sums enormous by those cheats are made,
> And deaths unnumber'd by their dreadful trade.[1]

Let us note the play on the word " Oxymel," and mark its significance. This chemical compound has two equal parts, and according to Dr. Arbuthnot, is a simple mixture, each constituent so diametrically different from the other as bitter from sweet, just vinegar and honey! Then watch the brevity in expression and condensation of explanation with regard to its contributory factors. Take, for instance, the partner, a clever propagandist or advertising agent, needed to make this physic known. His contribution is packed into one verse, or two linked couplets, where, in the six last words, we have the whole account of the sudden and unexpected result of the penman's collapse. What he had written so unmistakably caused " Oxymel " to sell, like our popular patent medicines, that it was bought up by the million; and immediately the fortune was made he died! Again, observe:

> With cruel avarice still they recommend
> More draughts, more syrup to the journey's end:
> " I feel it not; "—" Then take it every hour: "
> " It makes me worse; "—" Why then it shows its power: "
> " I fear to die; "—" Let not your spirits sink,
> You're always safe, while you believe and drink."

> How strange to add, in this nefarious trade,
> That men of parts are dupes by dunces made;
> That creatures Nature meant should clean our streets
> Have purchased lands and mansions, parks, and seats.

[1] " The Borough."

CHAPTER XII

> If after fearing much and pausing long
> Ye ventured on the world your labour'd song,
> And from the crusty critics of those days
> Implored the feeble tribute of their praise;
> Remember now the fears that moved you then,
> And, spite of truth, let mercy guide your pen.[1]

HERE, at Stathern, Crabbe composed some really
good poetry, probably resulting from a happier tem-
perament than at other times and places. In any case,
the last two examples are crowded with picturesque
and telling points—for instance, the skill in choosing
an appropriate name to serve the main purpose in
view. And, again, so many genuine little descriptions,
terse and graphic, contain examples of the poet's
shining wit—if the definition be accepted to mean the
joining of ideas by distant and fanciful relations so as
to give striking effects, or as Pope aptly puts it: " What
oft was thought but ne'er so well expressed." These
and similar illustrations prove how, after residing in
this neighbourhood, he had become an adept at
manipulating the mechanism so constantly employed
in the rhyming couplet of heroic verse.

There are, however, changes sometimes in the method
of treatment, especially when the theme is personal
and emotional in nature, and again we find him at
his best. Indeed, some critics consider the lyric compositions superior, others that his genius suited it
equally as well, whilst none proclaim it to be inferior.

---

[1] " The Library."

If anything, the lines are smoother and sweeter, both in expression and sound, more like the musical rhythm they are intended to represent, but the cool-headed, matter-of-fact Crabbe rarely used them; the exceptions are nearly always when he is concerned about the fair sex, as in a recent instance: " Come lead me, lassie, to the shade." The best is preserved amongst the " Occasional Pieces " with a familiar title " The Ladies of the Lake," and there is no question about the date —1785. The poem must therefore have been written shortly after a visit to these friends:

> Shall I, who oft have woo'd the muse
>   For gentle ladies' sake,
> So fair a theme as this refuse—
>   The Ladies of the Lake ?
>
> Hail, happy pair ! 'tis yours to share
>   Life's elegance and ease:
> The bliss of wealth without the care,
>   The will and power to please—
>
> To please, but not alone our eyes,
>   Nor yet alone our mind;
> Your taste, your goodness, charm the wise—
>   Your manners all mankind.
>
> The pleasant scenes that round you glow,
>   Like caskets fraught with gold,
> Though beauteous in themselves, yet owe
>   Their worth to what they hold.
>
> Trees may be found, and lakes, as fair;
>   Fresh lawns, and gardens green;
> But where again the sister-pair
>   Who animate the scene ?
>
> Where sense of that superior kind,
>   Without man's haughty air ?
> And where, without the trifling mind,
>   The softness of the fair ?

The biographer gives some interesting particulars by way of explanation. Normanston is the sweet little villa near Beccles, an early resort during Mr. Crabbe's and Miss Elmy's long and happy engagement. Here, four or five spinsters independent by fortune had formed a quaint Nunnery, the Abbess being Miss Blacknell, who afterwards deserted it to become the wife of Admiral Sir Thomas Graves. She was a distinguished lady, elegant in her tastes and manners. Another well-known Sister was Miss Waldron, from Tamworth—dear, good-humoured, hearty, masculine Miss Waldron, who could sing a jovial song like a fox-hunter, and, like him, I had almost said, toss a glass; and yet there was such an air of high *ton*, and such intellect mingled with these manners, that the perfect lady was not veiled for a moment. Now we conclude with the remaining four stanzas, in gentle and subdued humour befitting the theme, and consider that Crabbe himself, like Shelley, would admit that, whatever be the verse, good " poetry is the record of the best and happiest moments of the happiest and best minds."

Folly, with wealth, may idly raise
　　Her hopes to shine like you,
And humble flattery sound her praise,
　　Till she believes it true;

But wealth no more can give that grace
　　To souls of meaner kind,
Than summer's fiery sun can chase
　　Their darkness from the blind.

But drop, you'll say, the useless pen:
　　Reluctant, I obey,
Yet let me take it once again,
　　If not to praise, to pray—

That you, with partial grace, may deign
　　This poor attempt to take,
And I may oft behold again
　　The Ladies of the Lake.

Support for the opening assertions may be found in the poet's diary, under date May 10th, 1780, marking the beginning of the period when the mental struggle as well as the desire for Sarah Elmy's influential help is clearly perceived. For example: " I am now debating whether an Ode or a Song should have the next place in the collection." And again on the 12th: " Perhaps it is the most difficult thing in the world to tell how far a man's vanity will run away with his passions. I shall, therefore, not determine how far my poetical talents may or may not merit applause. For the first time in my life I have written three or four stanzas that so far touched me in the reading them as to take off the consideration that they were things of my own fancy. Now if ever I do succeed I will take particular notice if this passage is remarked (by the critic army), you shall rarely find the same humour hold two days. I'm dull and heavy, nor can go on with my work. . . . Oh, Sally, how I want you !" That Crabbe succeeded, after much searching of heart, with a theme scarcely touched upon by other poets, was afterwards seen by the wonderful attention, admiration, and sympathy aroused when the *Works* were published. For they contained true, descriptive verses on such rare subjects as the " gipsy " vagabonds. Therefore, we affirm that he did for literature, in his day, what Sickert, the inimitable artist, is doing for painting in our own—inasmuch as their unusual pictures have met with both a controversial and enthusiastic reception. Oddly enough, the poet possessed very little artistic talent, and never studied either music or painting. Being, however, very friendly with Reynolds, and accustomed to sit in his studio whilst the great Sir Joshua worked, he learnt something concerning harmonising and colouring effects, if nothing else. Still, what his son tells us is true, though at times hard to believe: " He had no real love for what a painter's eye considers as the beauties of landscape,

but he had a passion for science of the human mind
first, then of nature in general, and lastly that of
abstract qualities."

During these four years Crabbe wrote over 40,000
lines in heroic and epic verse according to his own
computation, and that is said to be the contributory
cause of much weakness; for, like Wordsworth, he
suffered from over-production, as well as inability often
to distinguish the differences of quality in the quantity.
Myra's helpful influence and criticism, however painful
it may have been for him to endure, added largely to
the brilliancy of this period's best composition. She
listened to it all, and pronounced judgment. Indeed,
a glimpse at the long-suffering wife's drastic pruning
may be caught in this reference: " Numberless were
the manuscripts which his father now completed, and
not a few of them were never destined to see the light.
I can well remember more than one grand cremation—
not in the chimney, for the bulk of the paper to be
consumed would have endangered the house—but in
the open air." The ones mostly preserved were those
familiar classical couplets, such as the general instances
already quoted; for he is supposed to be looking over
a few rural local productions whilst waiting here
for clerical preferment. Having, then, peeped into
this collection, studied the various subjects, their situations, surroundings, versification, etc., let us enquire
into the reason for these remarkably descriptive
pastoral scenes. In the first place, the poet had
previously arrived at the conclusion that the public
needed something besides pleasing and fanciful rhymes
like the gentle shepherd which had become so monotonous, chiefly because they wanted strong contrast.
There were no deep shadows in the overhead sunshine
of rural England. Should any dark clouds appear,
then they settled upon the metropolis and other large
cities with their slums and poverty, criminals, drunkards
and cheats. They rolled over such small country

towns and villages, as Aldeburgh, Croxton Kerrial, and Stathern. But had these no mean and lowly dwellings ? Could it truthfully be said that their inhabitants were free from the worst vices, and un-depraved, merely because they happened to have an Arcadian environment ? Possibly long ago, but now—

> Fled are those times when in harmonious strains
> The rustic poet praised his native plains . . .
> I grant indeed that fields and flocks have charms
> For him that grazes or for him that farms;
> But when amid such pleasing scenes I trace
> The poor laborious natives of the place,
> And see the mid-day sun, with fervid ray,
> On their bare heads and dewy temples play;
> While some, with feebler heads and fainter hearts,
> Deplore their fortune, yet sustain their parts—
> Then shall I dare these real ills to hide
> In tinsel trappings of poetic pride ?[1]

Venturing boldly upon the change as developed and illustrated on this first attempt, and meeting with general approval, Crabbe resolved henceforth to become a realist in the poetic presentation of country life. So his versification is not simply the composition of an able rhymester, for many write verse which con-tains little, if any, poetry. Dryden has truly said: " A poet is a maker, as the word signifies, and he who cannot make, that is invent, hath his name for nothing." The scenes we have depicted originated in the writer's mind, and are all real in one sense or another. Take, for instance, " Andrew Collett," the publican:

> His heroes all were famous in their days,
> Cheats were his boast, and drunkards had his praise,
> " One, in three draughts, three mugs of ale took down,
> As mugs were then—the champion of the Crown."[2]

Is it not recorded in the Latin tongue amongst the burials at Stathern, under date March 24th, 1727,

---

[1] " The Village."   [2] " The Parish Register."

how that Thomas Bugg, a notorious character, rather more disreputable on account of frequently drinking, as tipplers would say, "at one gulp," a six-pint jug of beer (*quatuor sextariorum*: a sextary measures one pint and a half)? This vessel (*vas*) kept at Belvoir Castle, used to be commonly called "Bugg's Pint." Again, with regard to "Oxymel," the story is founded upon well-known local facts. Crabbe knew undoubtedly that the Rev. Thomas Daffy, Rector of Harby, in the next parish, had, about the seventeenth century, invented a certain cordial or "elixir," for all the woes that flesh is heir to, and called it after his own name. Moreover, he had read the advertisement in the *Post Boy* of 1707 to the effect that just before his death the recipe was imparted to an apothecary kinsman in Nottingham, who sold the medicine to his great advantage. Subsequently, it seems, his sister wrote the following "puff": "Those who know it will believe what I (Catherine Daffy) declare, and those who do not, may be convinced that I am no counterfeit, by the colour, taste, smell, and operation of my elixir. To be had at the Hand and Pen, Maiden-lane, Covent-garden." We can therefore understand the sentiments of one who really knew, and thus expressed his indignation:

> Oh, great Apollo ! by whose equal aid
> The verse is written, and the med'cine made;
> Shall thus a boaster, with his fourfold powers,
> In triumph scorn this sacred art of ours ?

Crabbe continued to act the physician, as stated, and to mix his own herbs and chemicals. He could, therefore, very well look back, recall qualifications, and consider his present responsibility.

> Shall I, preserver deem'd around the place,
> With abject rhymes a Doctor's name disgrace ?
> Nor Doctor solely, in the healing art
> I'm all in all, and all in every part;

> Wise Scotland's boast let that diploma be
> Which gave me right to claim the golden fee:
> Praise, then, I claim to skilful surgeon due,
> For mine th' advice and operation too;
> And, fearing all the vile compounding tribe,
> I make myself the med'cines I prescribe;
> Mine, too, the chemic art; and not a drop
> Goes to my patients from a vulgar shop.

Finally, in dismissing the subject, the poet lifts his sledge-hammer satire to pound to powder Messrs. Daffy & Co., of Harby, Nottingham, and London.

> Our Quacks are gamesters, and they play
> With craft and skill to ruin and betray;
> With monstrous promise they delude the mind,
> And thrive on all that tortures human kind.
> Void of all honour, avaricious, rash,
> The daring tribe compound their boasted trash.
> Wretches with conscience so obtuse, they leave
> Their untaught sons their parents to deceive;
> And when they're laid upon their dying bed,
> No thought of murder comes into their head,
> Nor one revengeful ghost to them appears,
> To fill the soul with penitential fears.

Some think that, having broken away from conventional traditions, the poet would desire also to sacrifice the established vehicle of expression. There is no evidence, however, to prove that he did anything more than attempt to do so. The Johnsonian double line, founded upon classical usage, soon came to be the favourite model most constantly employed. Few traces of variation from the ordinary course can be discovered beyond the exceptions already mentioned under the Epic, and only one or two instances in blank verse throughout the many publications. It is true he had misgivings:

> But though to write be now a task of ease,
> The task is hard by manly arts to please.

> Sudden I find terrific thoughts arise,
> And sympathetic sorrow fills my eyes:
> For, lo ! while yet my heart admits the wound,
> I see the critic army ranged around.[1]

Had the author developed his gift in this latter direction, like Milton in *Paradise Lost*, or by adopting a different kind of metre, the critics would say Crabbe had forsaken the best style for something easier and inferior; then others would have surpassed where alone he excelled. No, the young artist actually painted his pictures true to country facts, and concealed few, if any, elements, in the difficult heroic couplet. This stupendous task can be understood only when we duly consider what is meant by including all the shade, as well as the light, within a small canvas, so that every ray radiates distinctly from each couplet without causing a blur, somewhat after the manner of leading Dutch artists. Besides its accomplishment becomes much harder when the painter purposely chooses unpromising characters, found amongst the very outcasts in humble life. In fact, he alone could properly paint the poor, as the result of experience and regular practice—thirty lines daily !

In his own words, and not forgetting Myra's assistance, he tells us:

> Studious, we toil, correct, amend, retouch,
> Take much away, yet mostly leave too much.

Other poets, like Thomson and Tennyson, have given us equally good pictures, but with greater freedom in versification and less exacting measures. Moreover, at best, nothing very uncommon can be detected in their otherwise beautiful compositions; for they deliberately depicted what everyone could see in lovely surroundings, not the unexpected. Still, unusual subjects are readily found, outside crowded town

---

[1] " The Library."

haunts, even upon the lonely lands and lanes of the country. Indeed, soon after Mr. and Mrs. Crabbe had visited " The Ladies of the Lake," the following scene of Bohemian life came into view. A rough sketch is made en route, and left for retouching, as well as pruning by the happy pair on returning to the Rectory. With regard to gipsies there is little need to add anything except that these gentlemen upon England's byways, parasites on other people's property, showed the same dislike for any fixed settlement or regular work, and displayed the identical spirit of licentiousness for over three hundred years previously, as they do today, and yet no poet has been able to give us a better representation.

> Again the country was enclosed, a wide
> And sandy road has banks on either side;
> Where lo ! a hollow on the left appear'd,
> And there a Gipsy tribe their tent had rear'd;
> 'Twas open spread, to catch the morning sun,
> And they had now their early meal begun,
> When two brown boys just left their grassy seat,
> The early Trav'ller with their prayers to greet. . . .
> Forth from the tent an elder brother came,
> Who seem'd offended, yet forbore to blame. . . .
> Within, the father, who from fences nigh
> Had brought the fuel for the fire's supply,
> Watch'd now the feeble blaze, and stood dejected by.
> On ragged rug, just borrow'd from the bed,
> And by the hand of coarse indulgence fed,
> In dirty patchwork negligently dress'd,
> Reclin'd the wife, an infant at her breast;
> In her wild face some touch of grace remain'd,
> Of vigour palsied and of beauty stain'd:
> Her bloodshot eyes, on her unheeding mate
> Were wrathful turn'd, and seem'd her wants to state,
> Cursing his tardy aid. . . .
> Last in the group, the worn-out grandsire sits,
> Neglected, lost, and living but by fits;
> Useless, despis'd, his worthless labours done,
> And half protected by the vicious son,

Who half supports him; he with heavy glance
Views the young ruffians who around him dance;
And by the sadness in his face appears
To trace the progress of their future years;
Through what strange course of misery, vice, deceit,
Must wildly wander each unpractised cheat !
What shame and grief, what punishment and pain,
Sport of fierce passions, must each child sustain—
Ere they, like him, approach their latter end,
Without a hope, a comfort, or a friend !
But this Orlando felt not: " Rogues," said he,
" Doubtless they are, but merry rogues they be;
They wander round the land, and be it true
They break the laws—then let the laws pursue
The wanton idlers; for the life they live,
Acquit I cannot, but I can forgive."
This said, a portion from his purse was thrown,
And every heart seem'd happy like his own.

Jeffrey, the foremost critic, said: " This picture is
evidently finished *con amore*, and appears to us to be
absolutely perfect, both in its moral and its physical
expression."

CHAPTER XIII

FROM STATHERN TO THE SEASIDE—JELLY-FISH WONDERS —A LITERARY COMPARISON

> There may the poorest with the wealthy look
> On ocean, glorious pages of Nature's book !
> May see its varying views in every hour,
> All softness now, then rising with all power,
> As sleeping to invite, or threatening to devour:
> 'Tis this which gives us all our choicest views;
> Its waters heal us, and its shores amuse.[1]

THE poet produced equally exceptional sea pictures, frequently under the most unfavourable aspects. But this latter point is by no means astonishing, for we rather expect it from one born and bred on a dull, bleak shore. He himself said, when settled in Leicestershire:

> No, cast by Fortune on a frowning coast,
> Which neither groves nor happy valleys boast;
> Where many cares than those the Muse relates,
> And other Shepherds dwell with other mates;
> By such examples taught I paint the spot,
> As truth will paint it, and as Bards will not.

To give instances, the chaplain, after attending his flock in the woods and dales of the Belvoir country, had, like most natives, an " intense longing to see the sea, from which he had never been so long absent." Accordingly, one summer's day, in the year 1787, he mounted his horse outside the stable and courageously undertook a remarkable ride to some place on the

---

[1] " The Borough."

BOSTON—THE RIVER, BRIDGE AND STUMP.

FRIESTON'S OLD INN.
(QUEEN CAROLINE).

facing p. 103.

vast exposed East Coast, beyond the low-lying ground
and river mouth near Boston—not unlikely Frieston.

> On rode our hero, counting all the while
> The miles he pass'd and every coming mile;
> Like all attracted things, he quicker flies,
> The place approaching where th' attraction lies;
> When next appear'd a *dam*—so call the place—
> Where lies a road confined in narrow space:
> A work of labour, for on either side
> Is level fen, a prospect wild and wide.
> With dykes on either hand by ocean's self supplied:
> Far on the right the distant sea is seen,
> And salt the springs that feed the marsh between;
> Beneath an ancient bridge, the straiten'd flood
> Rolls through its sloping banks of slimy mud;
> Near it a sunken boat resists the tide,
> That frets and hurries to th' opposing side;
> The rushes sharp, that on the borders grow,
> Bend their brown flow'rets to the stream below,
> Impure in all its course, in all its progress slow. . . .

Now, having referred to " the few dull flowers that
o'erflow the place," our bard proceeds to inform us
that the very face of nature is as " various as beaute-
ous," for everything that grows has grace.

> All are appropriate—bog, marsh, and fen,
> Are only poor to undiscerning men;
> Here may the nice and curious eye explore
> How Nature's hand adorns the rushy moor:
> Here the rare moss in secret shade is found,
> Here the sweet myrtle of the shaking ground;
> Beauties are these that from the view retire,
> But well repay th' attention they require.

Jeffrey, again, said on this subject: " A fen picture
is what few other artists would have thought of attempt-
ing, and no other than Mr. Crabbe could possibly have
executed."

Then, upon arrival at his destination, where " he

dipped in the waves that washed the beach "—which almost goes without saying—we are bidden to

> Turn to the watery world !—but who to thee
> (A wonder yet unview'd) shall paint—the sea ?
> Various and vast, sublime in all its forms,
> When lull'd by zephyrs, or when roused by storms,
> Its colour changing, when from clouds and sun
> Shades after shades upon the surface run:
> Embrown'd and horrid now, and now serene,
> In limpid blue, and evanescent green;
> And oft the foggy banks on ocean lie,
> Lift the fair sail, and cheat th' experienced eye.
> Be it the summer-noon: a sandy space
> The ebbing tide has left upon its place;
> Then just the hot and stony beach above.
> Light twinkling streams in bright confusion move:
> Then the broad bosom of the ocean keeps
> An equal motion; swelling as it sleeps,
> Then slowly sinking; surling to the strand,
> Faint, lazy waves o'ercreep the rigid sand,
> Or tap the tarry boat with gentle blow,
> And back return in silence, smooth and slow.
> Ships in the calm seem anchor'd; for they glide
> On the still sea, urged solely by the tide:
> Art thou not present this calm scene before,
> Where all beside is pebbly length of shore,
> And far as eye can reach, it can discern no more ?

In " The Lover's Journey " the hero sees everything at its best; in fact, finds beautiful sights—all along a dull monotonous route right to the place where the heroine resides—just because he happens to be in a joyous mood. He is at the height of happiness there in her company, and most reluctant when obliged to leave the next day. Crabbe, at the moment, can be said to love the sea as much as Myra, for he has reached his heart's content, and may be found, either gazing across the briny deep fully appreciating its manifold charms, or, like the thorough naturalist we know him to be, very carefully scrutinising several

wonderful living objects, as he tells us in the following
lines:

> Now is it pleasant in the summer-eve,
> When a broad shore's retiring waters leave,
> Awhile to wait upon the firm, fair sand,
> When all is calm at sea, all still at land;
> And there the ocean's produce to explore,
> As floating by or rolling on the shore;
> Those living jellies which the flesh inflame,
> Fierce as a nettle, and from that its name.
> Some in huge masses, some that you may bring
> In the small compass of a lady's ring;
> Figured by hand Divine—there's not a gem
> Wrought by man's art to be compared to them;
> Soft, brilliant, tender, through the wave they glow,
> And make the moonbeams brighter where they flow.
> Involved in sea-wrack, here you find a race,
> Which science doubting knows not where to place.

Here also is a sea picture exceptional in merit,
which Gifford, another leader of the " critic army,"
admires. He states, with reference to the contents,
that " they have never, as far as we can recollect,
been so distinctly treated of in poetry, and the versification of the lower part of the passage particularly
is brilliant, and has something of the pleasing restless-
ness of the ocean itself." Now, of all the animated
wonders of the sea, these uncanny little creatures are
perhaps the most singular. Often microscopic in size
and transparent in colour, though a few specimens
are fairly large, it is by no means easy to detect them
when swimming, except sometimes in the dark, when
they send out flashes of light somewhat startling in
effect. So the clammy, slimy jelly-fish, with its
dreaded nettle-like sting, despised by most persons, is
now selected as an object worthy the poet's theme !
Well, let us pause for a moment in order to compare
this subject with the beautiful description of the water-
snakes in the " Ancient Mariner ":

Beyond the shadow of the ship
I watched the water snakes;
They moved in tracks of shining white,
And when they reared, the elfish light
Fell off in hoary flakes.

Within the shadow of the ship
I watched their rich attire:
Blue, glossy green, and velvet black
They coiled and swam; and every track
Was a flash of golden fire.

O happy living things ! no tongue
Their beauty might declare:
A spring of love gushed from my heart,
And I blessed them unaware.

And when we place them thus, side by side, the whole difference between the two composers, and what they represent, can be seen at a glance. Coleridge, who belonged to the Romantic School, views his sea creatures emotionally, definitely emphasising their supernatural beauty and its effect on the observer. He describes dramatically. Crabbe simply sets out to arouse interest in these and similar living objects which are not usually considered beautiful, and this aim characterises nearly all his work. He tried just to reveal common things, not in any imaginary and dazzling light, but as accurately and faithfully as possible. Naturally, the other stinging fish or snakes are a bigger type inhabiting tropical latitudes, where they multiply profusely in great variety and colour, the latter effect depending largely from the point of view. Considerably less picturesque illuminations are witnessed on the dull East Coast only in the warmest evenings towards a late summer end. However, let us proceed, linger, keep a close watch, and then

See as they float along th' entangled weeds
Slowly approach, upborne on bladdery beads;
Wait till they land, and you shall then behold
The fiery sparks those tangled fronds infold,

Myriads of living points, th' unaided eye
Can but the fire and not the form descry.
And now your view upon the ocean turn,
And there the splendour of the waves discern;
Cast but a stone, or strike them with an oar,
And you shall flames within the deep explore;
Or scoop the stream phosphoric as you stand,
And the cold flames shall flash along your hand;
When lost in wonder, you shall walk and gaze
On weeds that sparkle and on waves that blaze.

The biographer has added an interesting note from the treatises of Sir David Brewster, LL.D., on the *Depolarisation of Light* and kindred subjects. "There are few phenomena in nature more striking than the luminous appearance exhibited by the water of the ocean, when resplendent and beautiful in the calms of summer. It has excited the attention of naturalists at all times, and led to much discussion. Some took for granted that this property belonged to the water itself, not to any bodies contained in it. Others considered that it depended on the same cause as the light emitted by the diamond, after exposure to the sun's rays; or supposed the sea water was endowed with the property of phosphorescence. More recent experiments, however, made a nearer approximation of the true cause by showing that the luminous secretion, attached to the mucus of certain fishes, was diffusible in water; even certain marine worms and insects were also alike; so that it was now admitted that some of the luminous appearances might be produced by these means."[1]

It is very likely that the last-mentioned littoral or seascape verses were composed on the spot, and, with others, afterwards polished up into the elegant, clear, but stiff style of the classical school. Such lines as those dealing with difficult scientific subjects could only be written by one who had previously studied them carefully and deeply.

[1] Ed. 1834., see vol. iii., p. 161.

In Coleridge's pretty little picture, an entirely imaginative production, according to Wordsworth, we have no fault to find, simply because he avoids all objectionable obstacles. His water-snakes actually had never been seen. Yet even so we should know nothing more from that poet's point of view. Crabbe, on the other hand, must give full details, with the result that part of his information, though often interesting, makes poor poetry. The general reader usually does not wish to be bothered by words in parenthesis, neither does he relish reference to such things as the refuse along the shore. Irksome matter-of-fact statements likely to irritate the ear or offend the eye are best reserved for common prose. Occasionally there seem some grounds for supposing that this and similar sketches made during holiday jaunts were not always shown to Myra, and so escaped the pruning influence. But let us conclude, for it is getting late.

> What time the moon arising shows the mud,
> What a shining border to the silver flood:
> When, by her dubious light, the meanest views,
> Chalk, stones, and stakes, obtain the richest hues;
> And when the cattle, as they gazing stand,
> Seem nobler objects than when view'd from land:
> Then anchor'd vessels in the way appear,
> And sea-boys greet them as they pass—" What cheer ?"
> The sleeping shell-ducks, at the sound arise,
> And utter loud their unharmonious cries;
> Fluttering they move their weedy beds among,
> Or instant diving, hide their plumeless young,
> 'Tis pleasant then to view the nets float past,
> Net after net till you have seen the last;
> And as you wait till all beyond you slip,
> A boat comes gliding from an anchor'd ship,
> Breaking the silence with the dipping oar,
> And their own tones, as labouring for the shore;
> Those measured tones which with the scene agree,
> And give a sadness to serenity.

CHAPTER XIV

In sweet repose, when Labour's children sleep,
When Joy forgets to smile, and Care to weep,
When Passion slumbers in the lover's breast,
And Fear and Guilt partake the balm of rest,
Why then denies the studious man to share,
Man's common good, who feels his common care?

OUR hero would be feeling very tired after his ride
and stroll upon the beach, and quite ready for a
night's sleep. He had left his foaming steed by
a large, rambling, ancient building in charge of an
ostler, the factotum at the only establishment likely
to accommodate him. And if, as inferred, Frieston
happens to be the spot, almost unmistakably described,
that house is there to this day, and alongside the road
which used to pass close up to the sea-bank, although
the shore is now more than a mile away. This " long,
old-fashioned hostelry, with a range of stables telling
of days gone by, stands under the shelter of the bank,
on mounting which you find a bench level with the
bedroom windows of the inn whence you look out
towards the sea " (Rawnsley). Here, then, the poet
spends that night.

All the comforts of life in a tavern are known,
'Tis his home who possesses not one of his own;
And to him that has rather too much of that one,
'Tis the house of a friend where he's welcome to run.
Large the domain, but all within combine
To correspond with the dishonour'd sign;
And all around dilapidates; you call—
But none replies—they're inattentive all;

At length a ruin'd stable holds your steed,
While you through large and dirty rooms proceed,
Spacious and cold; a proof they once had been
In honour—now magnificently mean;
Till in some small half-furnished room you rest,
Whose dying fires denote it had a guest.
In those you pass'd where former splendour reign'd,
You saw the carpets torn, the paper stain'd;
Squares of discordant glass in windows fix'd,
And paper oil'd in many a space betwixt
A soil'd and broken sconce, a mirror crack'd,
With table under-propp'd and chairs new back'd;
A marble side-slab with ten thousand stains,
And all an ancient tavern's poor remains.
With much entreaty, they your food prepare,
And acid wine afford, with meagre fare;
Heartless you sup, and when a dozen times
You've read the fractur'd windows' senseless rhymes,
You reach a chilling chamber, where you dread
Damps, hot or cold, from a tremendous bed;
Late comes your sleep, and you are waken'd soon
By rustling tatters of the old festoon.

This, undoubtedly, presents a good picture of the Frieston inn when Crabbe slept there, and something similar can be seen even now. Still, from an artistic standpoint, the small canvas contains several blemishes. Then let us note what others have to say, especially the " crusty critics of those days." The *Quarterly* expert rather unreasonably dwells upon the supposition that this description is far too graphic and real for the art's sake. He maintains that " the function of poetry is not to present any truth, if it happens to be unpleasant, but to substitute an agreeable illusion instead, in order that we may take shelter from the realities of life in the paradise of fancy." Another, Hazlitt, comes nearer to the mark, although he tears to bits all the best writers. He begins, however, by admitting the excellence of two poets in particular who were still living, and mentions them by name. " I mean Crabbe and Robert Bloomfield," the author of " The Farmer's Boy," with whom we are not here concerned, except to note that " the fault of his genius is that it is too humble, too rustic, and too menial !" He informs us that " Crabbe is, if not the most natural, the most literal of our descriptive poets. He exhibits the smallest circumstances of the smallest things. He gives the very costume of meanness, the non-essentials of every trifling incident. He is his own landscape-painter, and engraver too; has an eye to the number of arms in an old worm-eaten chair, and takes care to inform himself and the reader whether a joint-stool stands upon three legs or upon four. If a settle by the fireside stands awry, it gives him as much disturbance as a tottering world; and he records the rent in a ragged counterpane as an event in history. He is equally curious in his backgrounds and in his figures." Evidently what he says is partly true, and not altogether undeserving. But before passing final judgment and quitting " Queen Caroline " we might also observe what the latest authority on such subjects as these has to say. " Nobody using our inns three centuries ago found them romantic, and if they were not romantic then they cannot be now. Their architecture was as common to those eyes as the architecture of London gin-palaces is to ours, and sleeping in a carven four-poster as common then as sleeping on a Vi-spring mattress now. Nobody who travelled by horse or coach thought he was doing anything romantic, and he wasn't; he was using the best-known means of travelling, and he only put up for the night at an inn, not because he had any pleasure in inns, but because he had not reached his destination. That is why the old inn is so delightful in its atmosphere—not because it was cherished and consciously endued with interest in its time, but because it was a commonplace of every-day life, and developed to the natural needs and moods of man."[1]

[1] *The English Inn*, by T. Burke, 1930.

As a student, Crabbe was always a hard worker, often accustomed to burn the midnight oil when everyone else had gone to bed. In answer to the opening question we find him ready to sacrifice night's soft and " sweet repose " in order:

That after-ages may repeat his praise,
And fame's fair meed be his for length of days.
Delightful prospect ! when we leave behind
A worthy offspring of the fruitful mind !
Which born and nursed through many an anxious day,
Shall all our labour, all our care repay.

There can be little doubt that in these early days, under Burke's tutorship, the budding poet had a premonition of submitting his work to posterity, not only for light, casual reading, but also for thoughtful and critical enquiry. And we know he did indeed become a popular writer, as well as one who contributed considerably towards spreading general knowledge.

We write enraptured and we write in haste,
Dream idle dreams and call them things of taste;
Improvements trace in every paltry line,
And see, transported, every dull design;
Are seldom cautious, all advice detest,
And ever think our own opinions best.[1]

This confession, admitted in grand editorial style, indicates what the author himself felt when he began to think about his imperfections as a writer of distinguished verse. In reply Crabbe does not seem to be discouraged by those who are said to be not the " worst judges of literary composition." Besides their observations had the effect which they ought— " he took more pains, and tried new subjects." An old friend in those days of poverty and trial, Bonnycastle, the astronomer, said the poet " never suffered his attention to be diverted for a moment, but gave his

[1] " The Candidate."

whole mind to the pursuit by which he was then striving to live, and by which he in due time attained to competence and honour."

Therefore the above and subsequent lines are particularly valuable for giving us an insight into the poet's manner and method when writing, not only now but afterwards, if we except the dreams. Moreover, they show how sensitive he became to public opinion and also to the advice from his best wishers. Still, their judgment, especially Myra's, often carried weight, and so we may sum up very briefly the result of much deserving criticism somewhat as follows: After the publication of works thus described, many of their characteristic blemishes disappeared. Byron, who had great admiration for the poet, acknowledged that such subjects were " coarse and impracticable." Henceforth, we shall be able to note less objectionable detail in more pleasing pictures generally, but not always, and, sometimes, in spite of refinement, a lack of colour:

> " Has then some friendly critic's former blow
> Taught thee a prudence authors seldom know ?"
> Not so ! their anger and their love untried,
> A woe-taught prudence deigns to tend my side;
> Life's hopes ill-sped, the Muse's hopes grow poor,
> And though they flatter, yet they charm no more.
> Experience points where lurking dangers lay,
> And as I run, throws caution in my way.

At last the time has arrived for our hero to leave Frieston shore, and as his mood is now a ruffled one, the following scene of other days at Aldeburgh may have been recalled when looking for the last few moments upon the troubled water:

> All where the eye delights, yet dreads to roam,
> The breaking billows cast the flying foam
> Upon the billows rising—all the deep
> Is restless change; the waves so swell'd and steep,

Breaking and sinking, and the sunken swells
Not one, one moment in its station dwells;
But nearer land you may the billows trace,
As if contending in their watery chase;
May watch the mightiest till the shoal they reach,
Then break and hurry to their utmost stretch;
Curl'd as they come, they strike with furious force,
And then reflowing, take their grating course,
Raking the rounded flints, which ages past
Roll'd by their rage, and shall to ages last.

Here we may pause to note the complimentary observation made by Gifford: " A prospect of the ocean inspires Mr. Crabbe with congenial sublimity. This storm is detailed with a masterly and interesting exactness." The next few lines illustrate the pictorial effect caused by the introduction of bird life as a natural accompaniment:

Far off the Petrel in the troubled way
Swims with her brood or flutters in the spray,
She rises often, often drops again,
And sports at ease on the tempestuous main.
High o'er the restless deep, above the reach
Of gunners' hope, vast flights of wild ducks screech;
Far as the eye can glance on either side,
In a broad space and level line they glide;
All in their wedge-like figures from the north,
Day after day, flight after flight, go forth.
In-shore their passage tribes of sea-gulls urge,
And drop for prey within the sweeping surge;
Oft in the rough opposing blast they fly
Far back, then turn, and all their force apply,
While to the storm they give their weak, complaining cry;
Or clap the sleek white pinion to the breast,
And in the restless ocean dip for rest.

Again, the same admirer adds: " The imposing tumult of these scenes scarcely permits us to remark how the grandeur of the subject is supported by that of the verse !" So it may be taken for granted that

both subject and versification are now quite satisfactory, and he can justly exclaim:

> Thus as on fatal floods to fame I steer,
> I dread the storm that ever rattles here
> Nor think enough, that long my yielding soul
> Has felt the Muse's soft but strong control,
> Nor think enough that manly strength and ease,
> Such as have pleased a friend, will strangers please;
> But, suppliant, to the critic's throne I bow,
> Here burn my incense, and here pay my vow.

Now, however, the return has begun, and we may
proceed to trace the rider somewhere along the Witham
banks near Boston.

> Forth rode our hero by the river's side,
> Inland and winding, smooth, and full, and wide,
> That roll'd, majestic, on, in one soft-flowing tide;
> The road, now near, now distant, winding led
> By lovely meadows which the waters fed.

But the rich, fertile lands of the fens almost ripe
for harvest, had lost their fascinating interest after
visiting the beloved sea.

> " I hate these scenes," our hero angry cried,
> " And these proud farmers ! yes, I hate their pride.
> See ! that slack fellow, how he strides along,
> Strong as an ox, and ignorant as strong;
> Can yon close crops a single eye detain
> But he who counts the profit of the grain ?
> And these vile beans with deleterious smell,
> Where is their beauty ? Can a mortal tell ?"

Then, still feeling much in the same humour,
Grantham suddenly comes into view.

> Our trav'ller, lab'ring up a hill, look'd down
> Upon a lively, busy, pleasant town;
> All he beheld were there alert, alive,
> The busiest bees that ever stock'd a hive.

An allusion to Castlegate's "Beehive Inn":

> Stop, traveller, this wondrous sign explore,
> And say when thou hast view'd it o'er and o'er
> Grantham now two rareties are thine,
> A lofty steeple and a living sign.

There is a wedding; he hears the bells of Saint Wulfram, but sarcastically enquires and answers hurriedly at one and the same time:

> What are this foolish mirth, these idle joys?
> Attempts to stifle doubt and fear by noise.

But Stathern is not far off.

> And now approaching to the Journey's end,
> His anger fails, his thoughts to kindness tend,
> Now gently rising, hope contends with doubt,
> And casts a sunshine on the views without;
> And still reviving joy and lingering gloom
> Alternate empire o'er his soul assume;
> Till long perplex'd, he now began to find
> The softer thoughts engross the settling mind;
> He saw the Rect'ry, and should quickly see
> His Myra's self—and angry could he be?
> No! the resentment melted all away.

Photo.

Walter Lee.

THE CASTLEGATE, GRANTHAM.

facing p. 116.

CHAPTER XV

> Genius is jealous; I have heard of some
> Who, if unnoticed, grow perversely dumb;
> Nay, different talents would their envy raise,
> Poets have sicken'd at a dancer's praise;
> And one, the happiest writer of his time,
> Grew pale at hearing Reynolds was sublime,
> That Rutland's Duchess wore a heavenly smile,
> " And I," said he, " neglected all the while."[1]

THESE lines were jotted down during a certain visit
to Sir Joshua's studio whilst Crabbe watched him at
work, and listened to his reminiscences on Goldsmith's peculiarities. Indeed, the great painter was
then engaged upon the portraits of the ducal pair,
ordered at two hundred guineas apiece, only to decorate
the walls at Belvoir Castle for a few years and perish
in the fire of 1816. The words thus recorded are
interesting, first because they testify to a kindred
characteristic in the genius of our poet, and secondly
for the illuminating touch upon the personality of a
leading political hostess, who contributed in no slight
degree to his preferment, despite his unfavourable
views and gloomy misgivings.

Now, having dealt with the curacy-in-charge, we
proceed to the next important change in Mr. Crabbe's
life. This happened through the widowed Duchess,
Lady Mary Isabella Somerset, the Duke of Beaufort's
daughter, who was noted for her bewitching beauty
and " Tory " influence, just in the same way as the

[1] " The Patron."

Duchess of Devonshire amongst the " Whigs " of that Parliamentary period.   The chaplain belonged to the latter party.   In some of the practical and undignified jokes played upon him he rather distrusted the artful machinations designed by the laughing Duchess, for

> With th' amusement pleased, of conquest vain,
> She seeks her pleasure, careless of thy pain;
> She gives thee praise to humble and confound,
> Smiles to ensnare, and flatters thee to wound.

Like other beautiful and powerful women, her special weaknesses were seen to be vanity and selfishness—a case of painting the lily and leaving the Duke to take care of himself.   The " Historical MSS. Commission," based upon letters found at Belvoir some years ago, throws much light upon these points.   We quote a few short sentences from correspondence during the Lord-Lieutenancy, when the Duke resided at Dublin and his wife in London, because she detested the Irish: " 1784, *March* 17*th*.—The Duchess of Rutland does the Cabinet the honour of giving them a dinner on Friday."   " *April* 3*rd*.—Lord Stamford writes to complain of the Duchess having canvassed votes for Mr. Macnamara for the Borough of Leicester."   " *May* 6*th*.—The Duchess has a bet with the Prince of Wales over the election of Fox, a Member for Westminster."   And in the same letter we have a reference to both ladies, who are bent on outdoing each other. Daniel Pulteney writes: " You have seen by the English papers about the Duchess of Devonshire's canvass. Some say she carried matters too far, and may be brought before a Committee for bribery.   I hear of instances in the Cambridge election where the Duchess of Rutland's orders had a very good effect, though without a bribe."   That seems like currying favour, and, in light of the Leicester complaint, suspicious. Then, three years later, 1787, *June* 15*th*, the Lord-Lieutenant had unexpectedly observed certain changes

in his wife's complexion as well as demeanour towards
their constituents—

> Fled is the charming bloom that nature spread
> Upon her cheek, the pure, the rosy red—
> This and the look serene, the calm, kind look are fled.
> Sorrow and sadness now the place possess,
> And the pale cast of anxious fretfulness.

Moreover, having noted that the methods adopted
to colour the one and improve the other had been
overdone, the husband stated, " I was at the play last
night"; and speaking of a friend, who was also there,
informed his wife, " She wears but very little rouge.
. . . I wish I may be able to make you believe so. I
detest it put on without mercy." And on " *June 29th.*—
If you meet any of the Irish, either at Tun-
bridge or at Spa, pray be particularly attentive to
them (even though they be twaddlers), a set of unfortunate people whom you hold in such utter contempt." Again, just before the Viceroy's death in the
following October, he expressed a wish to see his wife,
but added to Dr. Quin: " In point of time it will be
impossible; I must, therefore, be content to die with
her image before my mind's eye." Meanwhile—

> Her husband grieved, and o'er his spirits came
> Gloom; and disease attack'd his slender frame.
> Grief and confusion seized him in the day,
> And the night pass'd in agony away:
> " Would she were come !"—but still he shifted on,
> Till health, and hope, and life's fair views were gone.

Then immediately afterwards the *London Chronicle*
states, " A circumstance which is to be highly regretted
is that her grace the Duchess of Rutland set out on
Sunday morning on the way to Holyhead," but it
proved too late !

The symptoms Crabbe undoubtedly detected in the
heart of this fascinating person can be seen in certain

poetical extracts as, for example, after the following introduction:

There are no passions, to the Muse unknown,—
Fear, sorrow, hope, joy, pity, are her own;
She gives to each the strength, the tone, the power,
By varying moods to suit the varying hour;
She plays with each, and vails in changing robes,
The grief she pities and the love she probes.

. . . .

Be this, or true or false, it is her praise—
She mourn'd correctly all the mourning days:
But grieve she did not, for the canker grief
Soils the complexion, and is beauty's thief.
Nothing, indeed, so much will discompose
Our public mourning as our private woes.
When tender thoughts a widow's bosom probe,
She thinks not then how graceful sits the robe;
But our nice widow looks to every fold,
And every eye its beauty might behold.
It was becoming; she composed her face,
She look'd serenely, and she mourned with grace. [1]

" The Duchess did not forget the protégé of her lamented husband. But, kindly desirous of retaining him in the neighbourhood, she gave him a letter to the Lord Chancellor, earnestly requesting him to exchange the two small livings Mr. Crabbe held in Dorsetshire for two of superior value in the Vale of Belvoir." How surprising, the pastor might well think, for, after former experiences, he had no hopes of favour now from either the one or the other. Could she possibly mean to help him ? This written communication, however, had not the slightest effect, for we are told: " My father proceeded to London, but was not on this occasion very courteously received by Lord Thurlow. ' No,' he growled, ' by G——d, I will not do this for any man in England.' " But he did it, nevertheless, for a woman in England, who, arriving

[1] " The Widow."

in town, "waited on him personally to renew her request, and he yielded." A tremendous triumph, over this stubborn man who was rough, indeed, but diamond-like. Crabbe had already benefited by his generosity, as previously intimated, and refers to him in his earlier works—for instance, "The Newspaper," first published in March, 1785, and dedicated to his Lordship from Belvoir Castle. Later editions contained not only the poem from which a few of our extracts have been quoted, but also notes upon "the splendid career of the great man," with the following stanzas by the poet Cowper, who had been formerly his fellow-pupil in a solicitor's office:

> Round Thurlow's, in early youth,
>   And in his sportive days,
> Fair science pour'd the light of truth
>   And genius shed his rays.
>
> Discernment, eloquence, and grace
>   Proclaim him born to sway
> The balance in the highest place,
>   And bear the palm away.
>
> The praise bestow'd was just and wise;
>   He sprang impetuous forth,
> Secure of conquest where the prize
>   Attends superior worth.

There is also a reference to the "seals," the badges of state. Now Edward, son of the Rev. Thomas Thurlow, Rector of Ashfield, Suffolk, was born (1732) in the same county as Crabbe, and that fact appears to have been the chief reason for his friendliness towards the young man when he went to breakfast at the lofty and magnificent residence in Great Ormond Street. At a later date he dined there and wrote the following significant lines:

> See that mansion tall,
> That lofty door, the far-resounding hall,
> Well furnish'd rooms, plate shining on the board,
> Gay liveried lads, and cellar proudly stored;

Then say how comes it that such fortunes crown
These sons of strife, these terrors of the town ? . . .
But what says our Attorney ?   He, our friend,
Tells us 'tis just and manly to contend.

On that occasion he received from him his first
rectorial preferment, the benefices mentioned in the
letter. No doubt on those visits the question would
naturally arise how did such good fortune befall
this once poor lawyer. We can trace the progress
somewhat as follows. Thurlow was educated at the
Scarning Free School, so liberally endowed by William
Secker in 1604, where he gained a university scholar-
ship, but on going to Cambridge was so fond of foul
sport that his College sent him down. This seems
to have brought the too playful bully somewhat to his
senses, for he afterwards became Attorney-General and
distinguished himself as a constitutionalist by " in-
flexibly maintaining the right of England to exert her
full might in dispute with the American Colonies."
For this great service to his country he received in
1778 a barony with the Lord Chancellorship. Our
poet has him in mind during the famous litigation.

But when by slow degrees the arts arose,
And science waken'd from her long repose,
When commerce, rising from the bed of ease,
Ran round the land and pointed to the seas,
When emulation, born with jealous eye,
And avarice lent their spurs to industry,
Then one by one the numerous laws were made,
Those to control, and these to succour trade,
To curb the insolence of rude command,
To snatch the victim from the usurer's hand,
To awe the bold, to yield the wronged redress,
And feed the poor with luxury's excess.
Like some vast flood, unbounded, fierce, and strong,
His nature leads ungovern'd man along.
Like mighty bulwarks made to stem that tide,
The laws are formed, and placed on ev'ry side.[1]

[1] " The Library."

The next allusion is to the " Great Seal of England," the specific sign of sovereignty, given to the chief lawyer in the land for custody, as the most competent person to look after it. Well, one night in March, 1784, thieves entered his house and stole the precious Royal emblem ! Some think the burglars were " getting their own back " at the expense of the surly and severe old Judge; but according to another statement they had been in the employ of the Whigs, about the time of the dissolution of Parliament, which so many Members hoped to avert. May it not have been a practical joke or bribe devised by some lady or another for her party ?

> Are there those, who ne'er their friends forsook,
> Lured by no promise, by no danger shook ?
> Then bolder bribes the venal aid procure,
> And golden fetters make the faithless sure;
> For those who deal in flattery or abuse
> Will sell them where they can the most produce.
> Such are our guides; how many a peaceful head,
> Born to be still, have they to wrangling led !
> With clews like these, they dread the mace of State,
> These oracles explore to learn our fate.

Anyhow, Lord Thurlow took particular care of the next Great Seal, by always going to sleep with it under his pillow ! Crabbe undoubtedly depicts this worthy character as a wily representative of the legal profession in " The Borough." For example, when referring to Archer we are told:

> He is still severe,
> Surly, though kind, suspiciously sincere;
> So much he's seen of baseness in the mind
> That, while a friend to man, he scorns mankind.
> He knows the human heart, and sees with dread
> By slight temptation how the strong are led.
> He knows how interest can asunder rend
> The bond of parent, master, guardian, friend.

So the most beautiful woman of high rank recently styled " Queen of Ireland," who, according to Wraxall, " outstripped all rivalry in symmetry, elegance, and dignity," having no need to use the artificial aids of rouge and powder, save, perhaps, as the poet says, to

> Restore the roses that begin to faint,

easily prevailed on the hardest Judge, the foremost layman in England, and proved herself to be Crabbe's friend. Indeed, another authority states: " Obduracy seems to have vanished at her presence like the violence of the waves before the face of Thetis." Thereupon the triumphal episode concludes with this reflection, happily expressed in a witty and epigrammatic couplet:

> These are the arts by which a thousand live,
> Where Truth may smile, and Justice may forgive.

MARY ISABELLA.

THE "BEAUTIFUL DUCHESS."

Sir Joshua Reynolds.

facing p. 124.

CHAPTER XVI

EXAMINATION, PRESENTATION AND ARRIVAL AT MUSTON RECTORY

> Fortune sends him forth
> To a rude world unconscious of his worth;
> There in some petty parish to reside,
> The College-boast, then turn'd the village guide.
>
> .   .   .   .
>
> In his mind's eye his house and glebe he sees,
> And farms and talks with farmers at his ease;
> And though awhile his flock and dairy please,
> He soon reverts to former joys and ease.

AFTER thus agreeing to the patronal exchange and consenting to make the presentation, several obstacles remained to be overcome. One referred to the necessity for academical distinction before any clerk in Holy Orders could hold those benefices, even if the Archbishop of Canterbury should approve. Satisfactory arrangements, however, were concluded with the authorities of Trinity College, Cambridge (who, proud of the young author, had entered the name of Burke's pupil and Rutland's chaplain upon their books), for an immediate examination at Lambeth, instead of waiting until the completion of terms. As a result, this dignified degree, "Bachelor of Laws" was obtained on January 10th, 1789, and recorded under the abbreviation, or "figures," "LL.B." In "The Borough" may be found such appropriate and ironical references as afforded by the following verse:

> Strangers no wranglers in these figures see,
> Nor give they worship to a high degree;
> Unlike the prophet's is the scholar's case,
> His honour all, is in his dwelling-place.

The promised preferment followed fairly soon, because we are told: " On the 25th of February, 1789, Mr. Crabbe left Stathern and brought his family to the parsonage of Muston." The two parishes are quite near, scarcely more than half a dozen miles apart—in fact, so close that the journey could be accomplished in an hour. Besides in each case the little villages lie underneath and are almost overlooked by the Castle. It is not unlikely then that the following lines were jotted down whilst on the way:

> Above he saw a giant tower ascend,
> That seem'd the neighbouring beauty to defend
> Of some light graceful dome—" And this," he cried,
> " Awakes my pleasure, though it wounds my pride."

From the concluding words and occasional like remarks, some have erroneously supposed that the newcomer refused to inhabit the official residence, and built the present Rectory. For this imposing, though rather stiff, red-brick Georgian structure stands in a position intended, so scandal says, " to prevent any view of Belvoir." But if so, then the stigma should be attached to the next occupier, a wealthy son of the poet's friend, Dr. Gordon, Dean of Lincoln, who required something more stylish and commodious for his family. True, Crabbe never forgot certain " painful circumstances "; still, as Professor Hutton justly stated, " there can be no doubt the poet, with all his ironies, had no such resentful feelings." The other one, constructed of neighbouring sandstone, with the front facing due south and possessing a more charming aspect, stood somewhat lower at the bottom of the gentle slope-

> Down by the Church-way walk, and where the brook
> Winds round the Chancel, like a shepherd's crook.

The landscape, then as now, was, in the words of the biographer, " open and uninteresting. Here were no groves, nor dry green lanes, nor gravel roads to tempt the pedestrian in all weather; but still the parsonage and its premises formed a pretty little oasis in the clayey desert. Our front windows looked full on the Churchyard, by no means like the common forbidding receptacles of the dead, but truly ornamental ground: for some elms partially concealed the small beautiful Church and its spire, while the eye, travelling through their stems, rested on the banks of a stream and a picturesque old bridge." Moreover, their garden front could be seen from the road, where in and out curved the carriage drive, and there, close beside the present wooden palings,

> Near that same house, with those green pales before,
> Where jasmine trails on either side the door;
> Where those dark shrubs that now grow wild at will,
> Were clipp'd in form and tantalised with skill,

the poet loved to plant his flora. Indeed, the Rector of Harby, who lived here during childhood, pointed out to the writer several herbs together with a large cluster of the once rare Irides (*Iris fœtissima*) commonly called "the stinking iris," which is traditionally considered to have been brought to this spot during the removal from Stathern and where it remains to this day. Mr. Furnival also referred to his father's discovery of a quaint horticultural instrument used for branding tools and bearing the initials "G. C." Moreover, one can still see

> An ancient tree that in the garden grew,

but whether it be the present weather-worn mulberry is uncertain. The narrow and shallow Devon quietly glides past the far east end, in accordance with the above pastoral description, and is particularly alluded to in the accompanying lines as

> That winding streamlet limpid, lingering slow,
> Where the reeds whisper when the zephyrs blow;

> Where in the midst, upon a throne of green,
> Sits the large lily as the water's queen;
> And makes the current, forced awhile to stay,
> Murmur, and bubble, as it shoots away.

Apparently a favourite site, again, grown over with high evergreen bushes, may be observed where the biographer relates: " The crown of the whole was a Gothic archway cut into a thick hedge, and many boughs, for through this opening, as in the deep frame of a picture, appeared in the centre of the aerial canvas the unrivalled Belvoir." Furthermore, the ecclesiastical or " glebe " lands, just under thirty acres, still belong to the Rectory, and are the same as those inspected soon after arrival, some next to the garden and outbuildings, the rest not far away. These fields were previously cultivated by the Rev. Francis Bacon, the late incumbent's father, who kept everything trim, ran the small farm with up-to-date machinery, and put to the test new scientific theories about land tillage and cattle-rearing.

> Far different he from that dull plodding tribe
> Whom it was his amusement to describe;
> Creatures no more enlivened than a clod,
> But treading still, as their dull fathers trod;
> Who lived in times when not a man had seen,
> Corn sown by drill, or thresh'd by a machine;
> He was of those whose skill assigns the prize
> For creatures fed in pens, and stalls, and sties.

That Crabbe himself farmed the glebe at least for the first two or three years as a hobby, and then, becoming weary, turned his attention more particularly to study, is the conclusion arrived at from perusing such lines as these:

> In books and men beyond the former read,
> To farming solely by a passion led,
> Or by a fashion; curious in his land;
> Now planning much, now changing what he plann'd.

Anyhow, there we may leave him for the moment in order to glance within the Rectory. It is recorded when the family arrived Mrs. Crabbe felt unable to give the home that motherly care and supervision which she so fully exercised in the other, owing to ill-health. A recent addition to the family, the third child within the past four years, had weakened her constitution, and although she recovered, it apparently marked the beginning of a complaint that is said to have returned periodically. The same authority says: "My mother was attacked, on the death of her son Edmund, by a nervous disorder, and it proved of an increasing and very lamentable kind, for during the hotter months of almost every year she was oppressed by the deepest dejection of spirits I ever witnessed in anyone, and this circumstance alone was sufficient to undermine the happiness of so feeling a mind as my father's. Fortunately for both, there were long intervals in which, if her spirits were a little too high, the relief to herself and others was great indeed. Then she would sing over her old tunes again—and be the frank, cordial, charming woman of earlier days." The poet thus describes his wife during the spells:

> . . . As these melancholy fits invade
> The busy fancy, seeks the deepest shade;
> She walks in ceaseless hurry, till her mind
> Will short repose in verse and music find;
> Then her own songs to some soft tunes she sings,
> And laughs, and calls them melancholy things;
> Not frenzy all; in some her erring muse
> Will sad, afflicting, tender strains infuse;
> Sometimes on death she will her lines compose,
> Or give her serious page of solemn prose.

Whether these lines ever attained to a high standard, and were worth while preserving for publication, is unknown. That the afflicted lady possessed no little literary talent, and assisted her husband on many occasions, has been proved. What we note, sometimes, is the difficulty to state definitely that certain Doric verses, discovered only rarely, were conceived by one and the same genius, when the style is so different in metre and rhyme. A case in point presents itself in seven stanzas, rather morbid but beautiful in nature, taken from "Tales of the Hall." The first and the seventh help to explain the mental condition. They also betray the feminine touch.

> Let me not have this gloomy view
>   About my room, around my bed;
> But morning roses, wet with dew,
>   To cool my burning brows instead.
> As flow'rs that once in Eden grew
>   Let them their fragrant spirits shed
> And every day the sweets renew,
>   Till I, a fading flower, am dead. . . .
>
> Oh! take me from a world I hate,
>   Men cruel, selfish, sensual, cold;
> And in some pure and blessed state,
>   Let me my sister minds behold;
> From gross and sordid views refined,
>   Our heaven of spotless love to share,
> For only generous souls design'd
>   And not a man to meet us there.[1]

But to return to the rector once more, it is assuring to be told: "This severe domestic affliction did not seriously interrupt my father's pursuits and studies" —a statement easily corroborated in the usual versification:

> Still much he hazards, there is serious strife
> In the contentions of a scholar's life;
> Not all the mind's attention, care, distress,
> Nor diligence itself, ensure success.
> Books cannot always please, however good,
> Minds are not ever craving for their food;
> But sleep will soon the weary soul prepare
> For cares tomorrow that were this day's care.

[1] "The Sisters."

But then from study will no comforts rise ?
Yes, such as studious minds alone can prize;
Comforts, yes !—joys ineffable they find,
Who seek the prouder pleasures of the mind;
The soul, collected in those happy hours,
Then makes her efforts, then enjoys her powers;
And in those seasons feels herself repaid,
For labours past and honours long delay'd.
No ! 'tis not worldly gain, although by chance
The sons of learning may to wealth advance;
Nor station high, though in some favouring hour
The sons of learning may strive at power;
Nor is it glory, though the public voice
Of honest praise will make the heart rejoice;
But 'tis the mind's own feelings give the joy,
Pleasures she gathers in her own employ—
Pleasures that gain or praise cannot bestow
Yet can dilate and raise them when they flow.[1]

[1] " The Borough."

CHAPTER XVII

> Errors and evil came in many a form,
> The mind's delusion, and the passion's storm.[1]

CRABBE devoted considerable time looking through old parchments and books committed to his care, both here and at Allington, with the object of finding inspiration and material for his various compositions, as we have endeavoured to illustrate on former occasions. Then sometimes it became comparatively easy to trace many incidents, but more often than not there would be difficulty in finding the slightest evidence as to identity whenever personalities were mentioned. A long-standing friend, Mrs. Leadbeater, once asked him about his creations, whether they were real, or merely made up? He replied that the originals were always in mind, " but I felt obliged in some cases to take them from their real situations, in one or two instances to change even the sex, and in many the circumstances." We have had already a few examples of such disguises, notably in " Thomas Bugg." Rarely, if ever, does the author depend absolutely upon his imagination. For in the above reply he continues: " I do not know that I could paint merely from my own fancy, and there is no cause why I should. Is there not diversity enough in Society?" Besides he proves over and over again that " truth is stranger than fiction." So, with regard to the following authentic story, written in characteristic satire, there is simply a

[1] " A Fragment."

footnote to the composition stating that " the wandering pauper was suggested by Richard Wilkinson, a parishioner of Muston, who every now and then disappeared, like some migratory bird, no one could conjecture whither, and just as his existence was forgotten home came Richard to be again clothed and fed at the expense of the parish."

Now all the reason by himself assign'd
For so much rambling was a restless mind;
As on from place to place without intent,
Without reflection, Robin Dingley went,
To this poor swain a keen Attorney came—
" I give thee joy, good fellow ! on thy name,
The rich old Dingley's dead—no child has he,
Nor wife, nor will; his all is left for thee;
To be his fortune's heir thy claim is good.
Thou hast the name, and we will prove the blood."
The claim was made: 'twas tried, it would not stand;
They proved the blood, but were refused the land,
Assured of wealth, this man of simple heart
To every friend had predisposed a part;
His wife had hopes indulged of various kind;
The three Miss Dingleys had their School assigned.
So high was hope—the failure touch'd his brain,
And Robin never was himself again;
Yet he no wrath, no angry wish express'd,
But tried in vain to labour or to rest;
Then cast his bundle on his back, and went
He knew not whither, nor for what intent.
Years fled—of Robin all remembrance past,
When home he wander'd in his rags at last;
A sailor's jacket on his limbs was thrown,
A sailor's story he had made his own:
Had suffer'd battles, prisons, tempests, storms,
Encountering death in all his ugliest forms;
His cheeks were haggard, hollow was his eye,
Where madness lurk'd, conceal'd in misery;
Want and th' ungentle world had taught a part,
And promoted cunning to that simple heart;
" He now bethought him, he would roam no more,
But live at home, and labour as before."

Here clothed and fed, no sooner he began
To round and redden, than away he ran;
His wife was dead, their children past his aid;
So, unmolested, from his home he stray'd.
Six years elapsed, when worn with want and pain,
Came Robin, wrapt in all his rags again;
We chide, we pity; placed among our poor,
He fed again, and was a man once more.
As when a gaunt and hungry fox is found,
Entrapp'd alive in some rich hunter's ground;
Fed for the field, although each day's a feast,
Fatten you may, but never tame the beast;
A house protects him, savoury viands sustain,
But loose his neck and off he goes again;
So stole our vagrant from his warm retreat
To rove a prowler, and be deemed a cheat.
Hard was his fare; for him at length we saw
In cart convey'd and laid supine on straw.
His feeble voice now spoke a sinking heart;
His groans now told the motions of the cart;
And when it stopp'd, he tried in vain to stand,
Closed was his eye, and clench'd his clammy hand;
Life ebb'd apace, and our best aid no more
Could his weak sense or dying heart restore,
But now he fell a victim to the snare,
That vile attorneys for the weak prepare;
They who, when profit or resentment call,
Heed not the groaning victim they enthrall.

The writer, searching through these said documents,
failed to discover anything more significant than the
name of "Robert Adkinson," among the accounts
rendered for payment by William Allan: Constable,
1692. But the register for burials under date July 11th,
1746, contains a suggestion: "Died William Blandley,
a servant man of Great Ponton. He was run over by a
loaded waggon in Muston lanes, which broke his left leg
and right thigh, and run up a mortification. N.B.—He
was riding upon the shafts, and fell asleep—a caution
this to all carters. He was buried the following day."
Allowing for poetic licence, then, did he happen to be

one and the self-same person? No allusion to the "keen attorney" could be found, but the poet undoubtedly knew just such a character, hence the accompanying explanation:

> But lives the man by whom such deeds are done?
> Yes, many such—but Swallow's race is run;
> His name is lost—for though his sons have name,
> It is not his, they all escape the shame;
> Nor is there vestige now of all he had,
> His means are wasted for his heir was mad;
> Still we of Swallow as a monster speak,
> A hard, bad man, who prey'd upon the weak.

Crabbe also continued his nature studies, as elsewhere, at the earliest opportunity. For many results of his painstaking hobby were published shortly afterwards, as we have previously stated, in the *History of Leicestershire*. And that treatise contains several references to plants discovered in this district, with their botanical titles and notes—for instance: "Anthyllis vulneraria, common kidney vetch, or lady's finger, at Muston, Allington, etc." But, although better known in this connection, his knowledge extended into the animal kingdom and included geology and mineralogy where associated, as with the little creatures of the East Coast.

> He knew the plants, in mountain, wood, or mead,
> He knew the worms that on the foliage feed:
> Knew the small tribes that 'scape the careless eye,
> The plant's disease that breeds the embryo-fly;
> And the small creatures who on bark or bough
> Enjoy their changes, changed we know not how.[1]

Then the smaller they and their habitations were, the more pleasing the investigations became when examined through the microscope. Indeed, the son tells how the father could be found constantly sitting "absorbed in the arrangement of his minerals, shells, and insects;

[1] "Tales of the Hall."

especially 'fungi' and 'petrifactions.'" As an entomologist, therefore, at the quiet and secluded home, in
what is sometimes affectionately termed "The Cot"
by the Devon, he requests us to

> Think of me thus disposed, and think me then
> Retired from crowded streets and busy men,
> In a neat cottage, by the sweetest stream,
> That ever warbled in a poet's dream.

Well, one of these fascinating studies concerned both
animal and vegetable substances taken from the beautiful building of St. John the Baptist, opposite, the oldest
portion of which is the Early English tower with plain
pinnacles, pointed windows, and broached spire, containing a peal of bells in two pairs, placed above each
other, and inscribed: (1) IHS Maria; (2) God save the
Church and Regime and send us peace in Christ,
Amen; (3) Jhesus be our Speed; (4) All men that hear
my mournful sound, repent before you lye in ground
(1601). In descriptive lines on "The Church," we are
invited to make a particular inspection of the west-end
weather-stains

> Which Nature's hand alone
> Profuse of life, pours forth upon the stone
> For ever growing: where the common eye
> Can but the bare and rocky bed descry;
> There science loves to trace her tribes minute,
> The juiceless foliage, and the tasteless fruit;
> There she perceives them round the surface creep,
> And while they meet, their due distinction keep;
> Mix'd but not blended; each its name retains,
> And these are Nature's ever-during stains.

An apologetic explanation follows in prose. It is
quoted not only for the purpose intended, but also as an
example of the writer's characteristic style: "Nothing,
I trust, in this and the preceding paragraph, which relates to the imitation of what are called weather-stains

MUSTON CHURCH.
TOWER AND BELFRY.

facing p. 136.

on buildings, will seem to any invidious, or offensive. I wished to make a comparison between those minute and curious bodies which cover the surface of some edifices and those kinds of stains which are formed of boles and ochres, and laid on with a brush. Now, as the work of time cannot be anticipated in such cases, it may be very judicious to have recourse to such expedients as will give to a recent structure the venerable appearance of antiquity; and in this case, though I might still observe the vast difference between the living varieties of nature and the distant imitation of the artist, yet I could not forbear to make use of his dexterity, because he could not clothe my freestone with *mucor*, *lichen* and *byssus*."

> And would'st thou, Artist ! with thy tints and brush
> Form shadows like these ?   Pretender, where thy blush ?
> In three short hours shall thy presuming hand
> Th' effect of three slow centuries command ?
> Thou may'st thy various greens and greys contrive;
> They are not Lichens, nor like ought alive;
> But yet proceed, and when thy tints are lost,
> Fled in the shower, or crumbled by the frost;
> When all thy work is done away as clean
> As if thou never spread'st thy grey and green;
> Then may'st thou see how Nature's work is done,
> How slowly true she lays her colours on;
> And so embodied with the rock, that few
> Can the small germ upon the substance view.

It is stated that Mr. Crabbe called upon the Rev. J. Kendall, Rector of Barrowby, early in 1789, and he had shown him an imitation on his own walls, which in the judgment of some, appears preferable to the actual *mucor*, etc.   However that may be, the naturalist proceeds to inform us:

> Seeds, to our eyes invisible, will find
> On the rude rock the bed that fits their kind:
> There, in the rugged soil, they safely dwell,
> Till showers and snows the subtil atoms swell:

And spread th' enduring foliage; then we trace
The freckled flower upon the flinty base;
These all increase, till in unnoticed years
The stony tower as grey with age appears;
With coats of vegetation, thinly spread,
Coat above coat, the living on the dead:
These then dissolve to dust, and make a way
For bolder foliage, nursed by their decay;
The long-enduring ferns in time will all
Die, and depose their dust upon the wall;
Where the wing'd seed may rest till many a flower
Shows Flora's triumph o'er the falling tower.

Travellers with world-wide experience often remark
that they know no other country where Time tints
and tones stones, like those of our ancient parish
churches, as it does in England. A lovely soft grey,
with deep yellow colour resulting from age and vegetation, is by no means the least charm about this and
other little towers in the Vale.

CHAPTER XVIII

DIBBLE, MUSTON'S PARISH CLERK, ON FOUR SUCCESSIVE
RECTORS—IN AND OUT OF ALLINGTON—TWO OR
THREE MARRIAGES

. . . But hark ! e'en now I hear
The bell of death and know not whose to fear:
Our farmers all, and all our hinds are well,
In no man's cottage danger seemed to dwell;
Yet death of man proclaims these heavy chimes
For thrice they sound, with pausing space three times.
" Go, of my Sexton seek whose days are sped ?
What ! he, himself !—and is old Dibble dead ?"[1]

NICHOLS gives January 9th, 1789, as the date of Crabbe's
institution, and adds this note of commendation: " It
would be an injustice to pass over in total silence the name
of a gentleman whose poetical talents are the least part
of his praise.   But I should offend if I were to say more
on this subject than that I have for many years experienced his friendship, and that his communications
in the progress of this laborious work are such as en-
title him to my warmest and most grateful acknowledg-
ments."   We may thus infer that in spite of his patron's
death, Myra's malady, and other professional and
domestic troubles, the chaplain and pastor had been
diligent in supplying much information in connection
with the Vale of Belvoir generally.   Quite naturally,
then, he would try to discover the leading characteristic
of his immediate predecessors, by questioning the parish
clerk, especially as he happened to have held the office
for more than half a century.   They had worked together only a short time when the newly appointed in-

[1] " The Parish Register."

cumbent bids us listen to the passing bell (number four
with its " doleful sound "). He recognised its notes,
and, having heard the startling news, doubtless remembered the warning:

> Yes, he is gone; and we are going all;
> Like flowers we wither, and like leaves we fall.
> So, Dibble's gone; his care and skill I lose,
> And gain a mournful subject for my muse;
> His masters lost, he'd oft in turn deplore,
> And kindly add: " Heaven grant I lose no more !"
> Yet while he spake, a sly and pleasant glance
> Appear'd at variance with his complaisance;
> For as he told their fate and varying worth,
> He archly look'd,—" I yet may bear thee forth."

Little else is known of this hale body than here recorded in quaint and sombre humour except that " his
eightieth year he reached still undecayed." The poet,
however, is not concerned with Dibble's own career,
but just calls him to mind for a few moments in order
that he may introduce us to four Rectors of Muston.

> " When first " (Dibble began) " my trade I plied,
> Good Master Addle was the parish guide;
> His Clerk and Sexton, I beheld with fear,
> His stride majestic, and his frown severe;
> A noble pillar of the Church he stood
> Adorned with College gown and parish hood;
> Then as he paced the hallow'd aisles about,
> He filled the sevenfold surplice fairly out !
> But in his pulpit, wearied down with prayer,
> He sat and seem'd as in his study chair;
> For while the anthem swell'd and when it ceased,
> Th' expecting people view'd their slumbering priest;
> Who, dozing, died——"

Sketch number one ends as here indicated by a dash
before the line is spanned, and depicts the deportment
of the Rev. Samuel North, appointed to the Rectory,

on January 24th, 1738.   This clerical magnate has been
likened to Fielding's " Parson Trulliber " in most
respects.   If so, Dibble had good reason to fear Master
Addle, " one of the largest men you should see, and
could have acted the part of Sir John Falstaff without
stuffing.   Add to this the rotundity of his belly, which
was considerably increased by the shortness of his
stature, his shadow ascending very near as far in height
when he lay on his back as when he stood on his legs.
His voice was loud and hoarse, and his accent extremely
broad.   To complete the whole, he had a stateliness in
his gait when he walked not unlike that of a goose, only
he stalked slower."   Mr. North was buried on March
28th, 1758, in the chancel, where a flat stone bearing
his name may be found.

> Our Parson Peele was next.
> " I will not spare you," was his favourite text:
> Nor did he spare, but raised them many a pound:
> E'en me he mulct for my poor rood of ground;
> Yet cared he nought, but with a gibing speech,
> "What should I do," quoth he, " but what I preach?"
> His piercing jokes (and he'd a plenteous store)
> Were daily offer'd both to rich and poor:
> His scorn, his love, in playful words he spoke;
> His pity, praise, and promise were a joke:
> But though so young and blest with spirits high,
> He died as grave as any judge could die.
> The strong attack subdued his lively powers——

The second portrays a trait in the character of the
Rev. Francis Bacon, M.A., that shrewd, business-like
man, who succeeded on April 26th, and straight away
began to raise the living in value, most likely through
the Enclosures Acts.   He started to improve the glebe
on lines similar to a home farm, but did not live long
enough to reap the full benefit of his labours, for quite
early in life apoplexy got hold of him, with the result
thus described:

" His was the grave, and Doctor Grandspear ours.
Then were there golden times the village round;
In his abundance all appear'd t' abound;
Liberal and rich, a plenteous board he spread,
E'en cool Dissenters at his table fed;
Who wish'd and hoped—and thought a man so kind
A way to Heaven, though not their own, might find.
To them, to all, he was polite and free,
Kind to the poor, and ah ! most kind to me !
' *Ralph*,' would he say, ' *Ralph Dibble*, thou art old:
That doublet fit, 'twill keep thee from the cold:
How does my sexton ?   What ! the times are hard;
Drive that stout pig, and pen him in thy yard.' "

In an appended note we are informed that these and
other couplets make up " a rough outline " of Dr.
Bacon, the poet's predecessor, who succeeded his father
on April 22nd, 1768.   Francis Bacon (junior), D.D.,
appears to have been a brilliant scholar who held
additional appointments such as the Mastership at the
Grammar School of King Edward the Sixth in the
neighbouring town, which increased his income by at
least £200, together with the benefice of Allington
similar in value.   The facts that these posts were under
Crown patronage, and both incumbents bore the same
Christian name as the distinguished Bacon, Lord High
Chancellor in the preceding century, are rather significant.   These two worthies came from Gainsborough,
settled down at Grantham, and were buried in that
churchyard, the latter on September 19th, 1788.

Then came the *Author-Rector*: his delight
Was all in books; to read them or to write;
Courteous enough, but careless what he said,
For points of learning he reserved his head;
And when addressing either poor or rich,
He knew no better than his cassock which:
He, like an osier, was of pliant kind,
Erect by nature, but to bend inclined;
Not like a creeper falling to the ground,
Or meanly catching on the neighbours round—

Careless was he of surplice, hood, and band,
And kindly took them as they came to hand;
Nor, like the Doctor, wore a world of hat,
As if he sought for dignity in that;
He talk'd, he gave, but not with cautious rules;
Nor turn'd from gipsies, vagabonds, or fools;
It was his nature, but they thought it whim,
And so our beaux and beauties turn'd from him.
Of questions much he wrote, profound and dark—
How spake the serpent, and where stopp'd the ark;
From what far land the Queen of Sheba came;
Who Salem's Priest, and what his father's name:
He made the Song of Songs its mysteries yield,
And Revelations to the world reveal'd.

On this, the last, the biographer states: "The Author-Rector is, at all points, the similitude of Mr. Crabbe himself, except on the subject of his lucubrations."

The proclamation concerning Dibble's demise in a rhyming couplet would hardly sound acceptable to a poet's ear if he came face to face, so to speak, with a serious fact in life—that it passes away.

No longer truth, though shown in verse, disdain,
But own the Village Life a life of pain.

Between these mournful events, however, are happier ones such as: joy-bells ringing at the birth of an heir, for a wedding or its anniversary, as the Rector, referring to his clerical experience, goes on to say:

I, too, must yield, that oft amid these woes
Are gleams of transient mirth and hours of sweet repose
Such as you find on yonder sportive Green,
The Squire's tall gate and Churchway-walk between;
Where loitering stray a little tribe of friends,
On a fair Sunday when the sermon ends;
Then rural beaux their best attire put on
To win their nymphs as other nymphs are won.

Allington, the other benefice, is situated just across the county border, and about two and a half miles away in flat, low-lying land stretching out towards Foston, thus marking the northern limit of the Vale. The village has the distinction to be named in Domesday-Book amongst the earliest manors and churches in Lincolnshire, and always seems to have had a cluster of pretty cottages partly surrounding the common.   For in the same way as before the Conquest, so there is now an " Esquire," " Hall," and " Park." Indeed, its varied history during many generations can be summed up sufficiently by the two well-known families, Williamson and Welby, and their equally unknown but highly respectable servants. For instance, inside a quaint and almost miniature church near the Norman chancel arch can be seen a marble monument of the last of these Williamsons, who had been High Sheriff for Lincoln in 1765.   He died three years later, and his widow, named Elizabeth, daughter and heiress of Robert Cope, of Spondon, Derbyshire, married Sir William Earle Welby, Bart., of Denton, by whom she had ten children to hand down the estates and titles.   The intervening gaps can easily be filled up by observing the other memorials surrounding the sacred walls.   Then from the preceding century records a certain Welby married, in 1633, Eleanor, daughter of John Williams, Esq., by whom he had seven sons and as many daughters ! Apparently they all lived very happily after their weddings, even if previously there had been exceptional misgivings.

Like other parsons Crabbe could affirm:

> We have our couples here
> Who hail the day in each revolving year:
> These are with us, as in the world around
> They are not frequent, but they may be found—

as the following two or three instances mentioned, amongst the marriages in the " Parish Register ":

There came a well-dress'd pair, who left their coach,
And made, in long procession, slow approach;
For this gay bride had many a female friend,
And youths were there, this favour'd youth t' attend:
Silent, nor wanting due respect, the crowd
Stood humbly round, and gratulation bow'd.

These spectators noticed, however, that the bridegroom
wore a worried look, and many of them would like to
have a satisfactory answer to the question:

Why didst thou grieve?   Wealth, pleasure, freedom thine;
Vex'd it thy soul, that freedom to resign?
But rest the motive—all retreat too late,
Joy like thy bride's should on thy brow have sate;
The deed had then appear'd thine own intent,
A glorious day, by gracious fortune sent,
In each revolving year to be in triumph spent.
Then in few weeks that cloudy brow had been
Without a wonder or a whisper seen;
And none had been so weak as to inquire,
" Why pouts my Lady ?" or " Why frowns the Squire ?"

Again, from the more staid and faithful domestics
at the Hall sprang a couple just as happy in their
wedded life as any blissful Welbys and their many
connections.

Yet not to those alone who bear command
Heaven gives a heart to hail the marriage band;
Among their servants we the pairs can show
Who much to love and more to prudence owe;
What if, when Rachel gave her hand, 'twas one
Embrown'd by Winter's ice and Summer's sun?
What if, in Reuben's hair the female eye
Usurping grey among the black could spy?
What if, in both, life's bloomy flush was lost,
And their full autumn felt the mellowing frost?
Yet time, who blow'd the rose of youth away,
Had left the vigorous stem without decay;

> Like those tall elms in Farmer Frankford's ground,
> They'll grow no more, but all their growth is sound;
> By time confirm'd and rooted in the land,
> The storms they've stood still promise they shall stand.

And lastly:

> For Lucy Collins happier days had been
> Had Footman Daniel scorned his native green;

but in this case there were no joy bells.

A recent incumbent, the Rev. M. B. Wynne, discovered that his predecessor used to ride a little black pony between the two parishes, and enjoyed putting it to the gallop to and from Sedgebrook.

A BOTTESFORD MONUMENT.

BOTTESFORD MARKET PLACE STOCKS AND CROSS.

facing p. 147.

CHAPTER XIX

> Yes, there are tales that would remove our doubt,
> The whisper'd tales that circulate about,
> That in some noble mansion take their rise,
> And, told with secrecy and awe, surprise:
> It seems not likely people should advance,
> For falsehood's sake, such train of circumstance;
> But let us something of the kind recite,
> And tell you now of Lady (Manners) spright.

SURPRISE has often been expressed that the poet made such little use of his patron's family history and possessions as subjects for versification, especially after living in the Castle and immediate neighbourhood for so many years. One reason already given had regard to his own ill-treatment by their domestic staff, probably because he knew the life below stairs only too well. And although direct evidence is seldom discovered for personal reasons, yet allusions are met with here and there to substantiate the fact. Indeed, a case in point concerns an afternoon engagement at Bottesford on Sunday, June 2nd, 1793, when, according to a manuscriptal note, he preached the same sermon as in the morning at Allington. So this particular incident enables us to know that Crabbe certainly officiated, and therefore visited that beautiful building which has acquired for itself the graceful title of " The Lady of the Vale." Then we ask ourselves, has he nothing to say about those wonderful alabaster stones in the chancel so aptly described as " a corner of Westminster Abbey " ? The answer may be found in these couplets:

> Now sad and slow with cautious step I tread,
> And view around the venerable dead;
> For where in all her walks shall study seize
> Such monuments of human state as these ?
> Then let us go and to a tomb proceed,
> Whose names and titles few attempt to read;
> Old English letters and those half pick'd out,
> Leave us, unskilled readers, much in doubt.

The most interesting family memorials refer in some way to the eight Earls.   Each has his effigy, and they are in historical continuity from 1543 to 1679.   One, indeed, contains a remarkable inscription, and stands up against the wall in the south chancel.   Having arrived there, we too can read, *inter alia*, how—" In 1608 Francis, the VI. Earl, married the Lady Cecilia Hungerford, daughter of the Hon. Knight, Sir John Tufton, by whom he had two Sonnes, both which dyed in their infancy, by wicked practice and sorcerye."

Besides the record, this multicoloured and quaintly gilded sculpture, under its lofty and huge canopy overshadowing six personages, including the two children, rather gives an observer the idea of *tableaux vivants*; hence the following reference:

> Behold these infants in the frame beneath !
> A witch offended wrought their early death;
> She form'd an image, made as wax to melt,
> And each the wasting of the figure felt;
> The hag confess'd it when she came to die,
> And no one living can the truth deny.

Crabbe doubtlessly had heard a full account of the tragic story.   Indeed, he must have read that small book, entitled *The Wonderful Discoveries of the Witch-crafts of Margaret and Philipa Flower*.   Apparently the mother, Joan Flower, " a monstrous, malicious woman," and her daughters lived near Redmile. But what had these persons to do with the household staff at the Castle ?   Why, the mother

> . . . was a servant fitted for her place,
> Experienced, cunning, fraudful, selfish, base;
> Skill'd in those mean, humiliating arts,
> That make their way to proud and selfish hearts;
> When with gross flattery she awhile assail'd,
> And then beheld with hatred when it fail'd;
> Yet trying still upon her mind for hold,
> She all the secrets of the mansion told.

And the girls were employed " to look to the poultry abroad, and the wash-house within doors." Complaints, however, about their bad behaviour no doubt very soon reached the ears of their mistress, who eventually discharged Margaret; and as a result all three hated the Earl and Countess. At last, " as malice increased, the noble family felt the smart of their revenge, for the eldest son, Henry, Lord Rosse, sickened very strangely, and then died, September 20th, 1613." About five years later (March 7th, 1619) his brother Francis suffered a similar fate. The principal charge against them had reference to

> A grey old cat his whiskers lick'd beside,
> A type of sadness in the house of pride,

known by the name " Rutterkin," possessed with an evil spirit, which sucked blood from the necks of human beings. The main points in the tragedy turned out to be true. The children were murdered, probably by poison, but evidently Lord Manners believed the deed or deeds had been done through witchcraft, seeing the inscribed words were partly his own composition, and the stone stood there " during his lifetime." But not without reason, for two of the culprits, having been first tried and punished at the market cross, eventually came before Sir Henry Hobart, Chief Justice of the Common Pleas, and Sir Edward Bromley, one of the Barons of the Exchequer. They confessed their guilt, and were executed at Lincoln on March 11th, 1619.

Living almost two hundred years after, the poet,

from past medical experience, naturally ridiculed the superstition, and therefore in any account from his pen we should expect to find something slightly cynical and humorous.   Behold, then, the Lady Cecilia in hot pursuit after the diabolical agent !

> Oh, that hag !
> 'Tis she the enchanting spell prepares;
> By cruel witchcraft she can drag
> My struggling being in her snares;
> Oh, how triumphantly she glares !
> But yet would leave me, could I make
> Strong effort to subdue my cares.
> " Hence, ye profane !   I feel a former dread,
> A thousand visions float around my head:
> Hark ! hollow blasts through empty courts resound,
> And shadowy forms with staring eyes stalk round;
> See ! moats and bridges, walls and castles rise,
> Ghosts, fairies, demons, dance before our eyes;
> Lo ! magic verse inscribed on golden gate,
> And bloody hand that beckons on to fate—
> Lo ! that chateau, the western tower decay'd,
> The peasants shun it—they are all afraid:
> For there was done a deed—could walls reveal,
> Or timbers tell it, how the heart would feel !
> Most horrid was it—for, behold, the floor
> Has stain of blood, and will be clean no more;
> Hark to the winds ! which through the wide saloon
> And the long passage send a dismal tune—
> Music that ghosts delight in; and now heed
> Yon beauteous nymph, who must unmask the deed;
> See ! with majestic sweep she swims alone,
> Through rooms, all dreary, guided by a groan
> To find a something, which will soon expose
> The villainies and wiles of her determined foes."

The Countess Cecilia played a prominent part in history when widow of Earl Francis, for she is mentioned in legal documents during the Rebellion as a " recusant," the greater portion of her private property having been sequestered to reward " deserving ser-

vants " of the Parliament. Her body lies in Westminster, but without a monument !

With further regard to these tombstones Nichols
says: " They are now kept neat and in fine preserva-
tion, but, as no attention had been paid to them
previously in the memory of man, they had suffered
severely by time, though more by an indulgence of a
bad custom which the children of the parish claimed
as a privilege of playing in the Church on Shrove
Tuesday." Then these figures looked like those which
Crabbe saw at Ab-Kettleby and Skeffington—

> Mangled and wounded in their war with time.

And there, as here, he might have heard a sound
echoing through the nave.

> Hark ! to that shout, that burst of empty noise,
> From a rude set of bluff obstreperous boys:
> They who like colts let loose with vigour bound
> And thoughtless spirit o'er the beaten ground.

Anyhow, in 1783 the Rev. William Mounsey, then
curate of Bottesford, " undertook to clean them from
moss, dirt, etc., and fix up such small articles as could
be found. Led on from smaller things to greater, he
renewed in the ancient manner all the carving that
had been destroyed, made new things appear old,
surmounted every difficulty and completed the repair.
In this work he employed more than three years, and by
this laudable exertion has merited equally of the noble
survivors, and of the lovers of our national antiquities."

It is reported that he soon afterwards received the
benefice of Sproxton-cum-Saltby (on the Belvoir estate)
and found its ancient Saxon cross in the former village.

The historian also adds that in the churchyard is a
stone representing a woman praying, but without any
inscription. They say it was laid down for a young
lady called " The Fair Maid of Normanton," concerning whom is a whimsical legend that playing at

ball on Shrove Tuesday some of her companions smote
the ball with such force that it fractured her skull and
thereupon (*crescit miraculum !*) out came a great number
of earwigs and she died on the spot. That literally is
the tale as told today. What foundation it rests upon
is uncertain. The earliest register contains this entry:
" 1597 Jan. Item XIIII day—There was a young
maid buried found in Normanton field." And a note
states: " The figure may represent some person long
before (this date), like one of the Rosses, removed out
of the Church, to whom vulgar tradition, which not
infrequently happens, has annexed a fabulous history."

Throsby, writing about 1790, rather corroborates
this supposition. He says: " On the floor lies a figure
which has been removed from place to place in the
Churchyard where the boys will have an opportunity
of treating the lady with more rudeness than she has
before met with." It now lies in the west corner of the
south aisle.

The cranium incident is evidently a myth, therefore
in " The Maid's Story " composed by Crabbe we can
hardly expect to find any reference to earwigs ! His
description, however, of a handy, charming, diminu-
tive damsel in domestic service accords more with our
expectations than any representation of a full-grown
person in a higher social position.

> Then from a secret hoard drew forth the Squire
> His tale, and said: " Attention I require—
> We had a little maid some four feet high,
> Who was employ'd our household stores to buy;
> For she would weary every man in trade,
> And tease to assent whom she could not persuade.
> Methinks I see her, with her pigmy light,
> Precede her mistress in a moonless night;
> From the small lantern throwing through the street
> The dimm'd effulgence at her lady's feet.
> What time she went to prove her well-known skill
> With rival friends at her beloved quadrille."

PARHAM HALL.

LINCOLN CATHEDRAL.

facing p. 153.

CHAPTER XX

> It was an ancient, venerable Hall,
> And once surrounded by a moat and wall.

TOWARDS the end of 1792 both parishes, Muston and
Allington, were left to a curate-in-charge whilst the
Rector hurried into Suffolk to execute the will of his
wife's uncle. For quite recently Mrs. Crabbe had lost
that well-to-do relative whom we incidentally met
during the long and happy engagement. The late
Mr. Tovell was an old-fashioned yeoman or gentleman
farmer,

> Who in large mansions live like petty kings,
> And speak of farms, but as amusing things.

He dwelt at what everybody called " Ducking Hall,"
but according to a picture in the South Kensington
Museum it is referred to as " Parham Hall, Suffolk:
the moat-house of the poet Crabbe." Certain particulars disclosed through correspondence preserved in
the " Broadley Collection " supply the dates between
his first arrival and the settlement in his native county
which covered the next thirteen years. For instance,
from a letter written by Myra at Muston Rectory,
containing the Grantham postmark of October 22nd,
1792, and addressed to Parham, we read, *inter alia*,
about the receipt of his message and her reply: " You
said, ' Expect nothing, my dear Sally '—from that
moment I expected nothing. But ultimately the
will may be a good one. It may be so, says I, after

reading it, for there is nothing so much left out of the family as I expected, tho' 'tis true not altogether to my liking." Then, after a short absence during which preliminary arrangements were made for their future accommodation, Crabbe returned home to pack up and fetch his family. Because the son states: " In November we arrived once more at Parham." Now at first he was well pleased and said :

> " These lands, this manor, all,
>   Now call me master !—I obey the call."
> Then from the window look'd the valley o'er,
> And never saw it look so rich before.

But a change soon came over him owing to some interference and annoyance from old retainers and others who benefited by legacies. Those chiefly concerned were the co-heiresses Mrs. Elmy and her sister, Miss Tovell (Myra's " Aunt Lizzie "). The latter lived in an adjoining cottage, and considered that everything should have been left to her own management. This lady, therefore, proved to be a thorn in the would-be farmer's flesh, for it is said she could " screw Crabbe up and down like a fiddle." In a certain composition styled " Procrastination," and evidently concerned with events in this and another household in the village, is a note saying that the sons have no doubt but that their mother's residence at one time with a rich old aunt, who was very partial to her, and abounded in trinkets, suggested the supposition of the tale which gives us an insight into the character of this imperial little woman, and also into her parlour.

> In small but splendid room she loved to see
> That all was placed in view and harmony.
> There as with eager glance she look'd around,
> She much delight in every object found,
> While books devout were near her—to destroy,
> Should it arise, an overflow of joy.
> Within that fair apartment guests might see

> The comforts cull'd for wealth by vanity:
> Around the room an Indian paper blazed,
> With lively tint, and figures boldly raised;
> Silky and soft upon the floor below,
> Th' elastic carpet rose with crimson glow:
> All things around implied both cost and care,
> What met the eye was elegant or rare:
> A silver urn with curious work was fraught;
> A silver lamp from Grecian pattern brought;
> Above her head all gorgeous to behold,
> A time-piece stood on feet of burnish'd gold.

True, so much property bequeathed to her passed eventually to him, but in the meanwhile the poet's thoughts can be imagined only too well, as he goes to have another look at the precious legal document on the first occasion when Lizzie " screwed her violin " a little too tightly !

> Again he reads—but he had read enough,
> What follow'd put his virtue to a proof.
> " How's this ?—to (Sister Liz) two thousand pounds !
> A monstrous sum ! Beyond all reason ! Zounds !"
>
> .   .   .   .
>
> So he is wretched for his fate decrees
> That his own feelings should deny him ease,
> And the strong sense that bids him to confess
> He has not found the way to happiness.

The reference in these last couplets is to the departure from Muston thus explained by his son: " It was a step reluctantly taken, and I believe sincerely repented of. The beginning was ominous. As we were slowly quitting the place, preceded by our furniture, a stranger, though one who knew my father's circumstances, called out in an impassive tone, ' You are wrong ! You are wrong !' The sound, he said, found an echo in his own conscience, and during the whole journey seemed to ring in his ears a supernatural voice."

Again, another annoyance is recorded which had to do with the farm-bailiff and poaching. Crabbe charged him with the fact. "The man flew into a violent passion, grasped a knife, and exclaimed, with an inflamed countenance, ' No man shall call me a rogue.' My father smiled at his rage, and said in a quiet tone: ' Now, Robert, you are too much for me; put down your knife, and then we can talk on equal terms.' The man hesitated; my father added, lifting up his voice, ' Get out of the house, you scoundrel !' and he was obeyed. On all occasions, indeed, he appeared to have a perfect insensibility to physical danger."

So disillusionment set in early, seeing that certain gentlemen like these made the situation rather uncomfortable. A parson and " Ducking Hall " failed to blend according to their notions. Indeed, they openly asserted that " Parham had passed away, and the glory thereof." On the other hand, no more poaching with impunity had a stirring effect upon the muse, because it brought the poet into close personal touch with several shady characters, who otherwise might have escaped careful examination. Through such actions he had, amidst an affection for husbandry, just that impetus which goaded him on, not only to thwart their designs, but also to multiply his couplets. Having, therefore, roughly sketched such individuals and their belongings, he strove to introduce them into sentimental themes (both rhyme and prose), in greater length than any previous attempts. The result of this elaborate and seemingly fictitious verse is rather poor as poetry, though often rich in real anecdotes. The author, conscious of the fact, refrained from publishing it during his lifetime; and the novels, meeting with Myra's disapproval, were burnt. Well, amongst the compositions concerning parasitical subjects rather affecting the agricultural community, two or three have their origin here, and are worth reading, if only for the sake of that association. Take, for instance, " The Dealer," Bonner, whose life is recorded just before the writer's departure from the Hall.

> Bad men are seldom cheerful; but we see
> That, when successful, they can merry be.
> One whom I leave, his darling money lends,
> On terms well known to his unhappy friends.
> He farms and trades, and in his method treats
> His guests, whom first he comforts, then he cheats.
> He knows their private griefs, their inward groans,
> And then applies his leeches and his loans
> To failing, falling families—and gets,
> I know not how, with large increase, their debts.

Thus the main design seems to concern Bonner's craft and wickedness, but one very distinguishing feature is the vivid description of the villain's dog—a cross-bred, wolfish lurcher, sometimes seen in the company of poachers and gipsies. That the squarson knew it intimately, and had sufficient reason for keeping the brute under observation, cannot be doubted.

> There watch'd a cur before the miser's gate—
> A very cur, whom all men seem'd to hate;
> Gaunt, savage, shaggy, with an eye that shone
> Like a live coal, and he possess'd but one;
> His bark was wild and eager, and became
> That meagre body and that eye of flame;
> His master prized him much, and Fang his name.
> His master fed him largely; but not that,
> Nor aught of kindness made the snarler fat.
> Flesh he devour'd, but not a bit would stay;
> He bark'd, and snarl'd, and growl'd it all away;
> His ribs were seen extended like a rack,
> And coarse red hair hung roughly o'er his back;
> Lamed in one leg, and bruised in wars of yore,
> Now his sore body made his temper sore.
> Such was the friend of him who could not find
> Nor make him one, 'mong creatures of his kind.

On October 17th, 1796, through further bereavements, the son says, " It became my father's very

earnest wish to quit Parham," and so he settled at
Great Glemham Hall, belonging to his old friend,
Mr. Dudley North, " where my parents remained for
four or five years to their entire satisfaction." Apparently Crabbe had been acting curate to this parish,
as well as Sweffling, a neighbouring hamlet, since the
beginning of 1794. Here he busied himself with the
education of his boys and usual clerical ministrations;
hence further contributions towards completing " The
Parish Register "—for example, " A noble peasant,
Isaac Ashford," whose " prototype we are informed
was honest John Jasper, the parish clerk of North
Glemham." At the close of the century the poet
sums up his own life here in " The Old Bachelor ":

> Six years had pass'd, and forty ere the six,
> When Time began to play his usual tricks;
> The locks once comely in a virgin's sight,
> Locks of pure brown, display'd th' encroaching white;
> The blood once fervid now to cool began,
> And Time's strong pressure to subdue the man;
> I rode or walk'd as I was wont before,
> But now the bounding spirit was no more;
> A moderate pace would now my body heat,
> A walk of moderate length distress my feet.
> " I show'd my stranger-guest those hills sublime,
> But said, ' The view is poor, we need not climb.'
> At a friend's mansion I began to dread
> The cold neat parlour, and the gay glazed bed;
> At home I felt a more decided taste,
> And must have all things in my order placed;
> My morning walks I now could bear to lose,
> And bless'd the shower that gave me not to choose;
> In fact, I felt a languor stealing on;
> The active arm, the agile hand were gone;
> Small daily actions into habits grew
> And new dislike to forms and fashion new
> I loved my trees in order to dispose,
> I number'd peaches, look'd how stocks arose,
> Told the same story oft—in short, began to prose."

In October, 1801, the property having been sold, the biographer continues: " We left this sweet place, and entered a house at Rendham, a neighbouring village, for the four years following." He is referring to an extension of licence granted to his father by the Bishop, who began latterly to insist upon the clergy residing in their parishes. And to understand how the dwelling became vacant so opportunely, we have to recollect that inhabitants along the East Coast feared Napoleon, much in the same way as many in our generation did the Kaiser during the early years of the Great War. Some left their belongings and fled, but Crabbe showed his pluck by taking over this smaller establishment and desiring to stay as long as possible, for his Lordship himself imposed the limitation. Again, he had no scruples in occupying a junior position under Mr. Turner, Vicar of Great Yarmouth, who proved to be a good and helpful adviser on all literary matters. Moreover, there are clear indications given that he would rather await the foe on the sea-front than forgo the realisation of his twofold ambition, which looked very much like being spoilt, when, fortunately, Dr. Pretyman, of Lincoln, granted this advantage.

> No, 'tis the infant mind, to care unknown,
> That makes th' imagined paradise its own;
> Soon as reflections in the bosom rise,
> Light slumbers vanish from the clouded eyes;
> The tear and smile, that once together rose
> Are then divorced; the head and heart are foes;
> Enchantment bows to Wisdom's serious plan,
> And Pain and Prudence make and mar the man.[1]

The first part of the plan concerned the careful tuition and successful home supervision for his sons' matriculation. Both boys, in due course, entered Trinity. The second, how to find the means of meeting that expense.

---

[1] " The Library."

Thus many more allotted months were passed at his native place preparatory to the publication of " The Borough" and some few "Tales." The accompanying quotations illustrate these contentions: "Cambridge, I was examined and entered, and in October, 1803, went to reside. When I left College for the Christmas Vacation, I found my father and mother stationed at Aldeburgh for the winter." Again later: " We happened to be on a visit (there) when the dread of a French invasion was at its height. The old artillery of the fort had been replaced by cannon of a large calibre, and one, the most weighty I remember to have seen, was constantly primed, as an alarm gun. One dark morning I heard a distant gun at sea; in about ten minutes another, and at an equal interval a third; and then at last the tremendous roar of the great gun on the fort, which shook every house in the town. After enquiring into the state of affairs, I went to my father's room, and knocking at the door, with difficulty waked the inmates, and said, ' Do not be alarmed, but the French are landing.' He replied, ' Well, my old fellow, you and I can do no good, or we would be among them: we must wait the event.' I returned to his door in about three-quarters of an hour, to tell him the agitation was subsiding, and found him fast asleep."

> Yes ! twenty years have pass'd, and I am come,
> Unknown, unwelcomed to my early home—
> The very place is alter'd.   What I left
> Seems of its space and dignity bereft;
> The streets are narrow, and the buildings mean;
> Did I, or Fancy, leave them broad and clean ?
> The ancient church, in which I felt a pride,
> As struck by magic, is but half as wide:
> The tower is shorter, the sonorous bell
> Tells not the hour, as it was wont to tell;
> The market dwindles, every shop and stall
> Sinks in my view; there's littleness in all.

Mine is the error; prepossess'd I see;
And all the change I mourn is change in me.
One object only is the same; the sight
Of the wide Ocean by the moon's pale light,
With her long ray of glory, that we mark
On the wild waves when all beside is dark.
This is the worst of Nature, and the eye
In vain the boundless prospect would descry;
What mocks our view cannot contracted be;
We cannot lessen what we cannot see.[1]

Lastly: " But the time was now at hand, that we were all to return finally to Leicestershire; and when in the year 1805 we at length bade adieu to Suffolk and travelled once more to Muston, my father had the full expectation that his changes of residence were at an end, and that he would finish his days in his own old Parsonage."

[1] " Farewell and Return."

CHAPTER XXI

Still I pass on and now before me find
The restless ocean, emblem of my mind;
There wave on wave, here thought on thought succeeds,
Their produce idle works and idle weeds;
Dark is the prospect o'er the rolling sea,
But not more dark than my sad views to me;
Yet from the rising moon the light beams dance
In troubled splendour o'er the wide expanse;
So on my soul, whom cares and troubles fright,
The Muse pours comfort in a flood of light;
Shine out, fair flood ! until the day-star flings
Her brighter rays on all sublunar things.[1]

HAVING given further records concerning the poet's connection with Suffolk, his life's history and work can be somewhat more briefly told. Crabbe's mind is still full of reflections after quitting his beloved Aldeburgh almost for the last time. Meanwhile, in 1807, " The Parish Register," " The Birth of Flattery," some other small pieces, and reprints from his earlier poems were published. Amongst these the most remarkable is styled " Sir Eustace Grey," a theme containing fifty-five stanzas, or about 450 lines. Browning called it a " Dramatic Lyric." The poem was composed at Muston Rectory soon after the return, during a great snowstorm, and apparently in one night ! Three years later appeared " The Borough," then, in 1812, " Tales," in verse. They all met with great success, for since so

---

[1] " Fragment at Midnight."

long an interval as twenty years, these efforts re-established an almost forgotten reputation, and as a result he began to enter once more into society, especially when the boys, George and John, had finished their College careers and became ordained. Thus the former states: " Besides the Castle, he occasionally dined at Sir Robert Heron's, Sir William Welby's, with Dr. Gordon, Dean of Lincoln, the rector of the next village (Bottesford), and others of the neighbouring clergy. And we now and then had a party at our house, but where the mistress is always in ill-health and the master a poet there will seldom be found the nice tact to conduct these things just as they ought to be. My father was conscious of this, and it gave him the appearance of inhospitality, quite foreign to his nature. If he neither shot nor danced, he appeared well pleased that we (the two curates) brought him a very creditable supply of game, and that we sometimes passed an evening at the Assembly-room of our Metropolis." These two phases are illustrated by the following verses, the first referring to Muston's old Rectory, already described:

> Our eager parties, when the lunar light
> Throws its full radiance on the festive night,
> Of either sex with punctual hurry come
> And fill, with one accord, an ample room;
> Pleased, the fresh packs on cloth of green they see,
> And seizing, handle with preluding glee;
> They draw, they sit, they shuffle, cut, and deal
> Like friends assembled, but like foes to feel;
> But yet not all—a happier few have joys
> Of mere amusement, and their cards are toys;
> No skill nor art, nor fretful hopes have they,
> But while their friends are gaming laugh and play.
> Others there are, the veterans of the game,
> Who owe their pleasure to their envied fame;
> Through many a year, with hard-contested strife,
> Have they attained this glory of their life.

The other allusion is to the old " Town " or " Guild Hall," Grantham, which towards the end of the previous century—*i.e.*, in 1787—underwent restoration and enlargement, not only to accommodate the Justices of the Peace with their various apartments, but also to provide a club or meeting-place for social purposes. This ancient building stood midway between the " George Hotel " in High-street and " The Duke's Yard," at the end of the thoroughfare still named after the Hall. Turnor, in his history (1806), says: " In addition to the sum of £1,000, or thereabouts, levied upon the town and Soke, for the above purposes, his Grace the Duke of Rutland, and the Right Honourable Lord Brownlow, gave £300 each for building a large room to accommodate the Corporation on particular occasions and to serve as an Assembly-room for the town."

> Next is the Club, where to their friends in town
> Our country neighbours once a month come down;
> We term it Free-and-Easy, and yet we
> Find it no easy matter to be free;
> E'en in our small assembly, friends among,
> Are minds perverse, there's something will be wrong;
> Men are not equal; some will claim a right
> To be the kings and heroes of the night;
> Will their own favourite themes and notions start,
> And you must hear, offend them, or depart.
> There comes Sir Thomas from his village seat,
> Happy, he tells us, all his friends to meet;
> He brings the ruin'd brother of his wife,
> Whom he supports, and makes him sick of life;
> A ready witness whom he can produce
> Of all his deeds—a butt for his abuse;
> Soon as he enters, has the guests espied,
> Drawn to the fire, and to the glass applied—
> " Well, what's the subject ?   What are you about ?
> The news, I take it—come, I'll help you out:"—
> And then, without one answer, he bestows
> Freely upon us all he hears and knows;

Gives us opinions, tells us how he votes;
Recites the speeches, adds to them his notes;
And gives old ill-told tales for new-born anecdotes;
Yet cares he nothing what we judge or think,
Our only duty's to attend and drink;
At length, admonish'd by his gout, he ends
The various speech, and leaves at peace his friends;
But now, alas ! we've lost the pleasant hour,
And wisdom flies from wine's superior power.

.   .   .   .

Till fuddled Friendship vows esteem and weeps,
And jovial Folly drinks and sings and sleeps.

We may possibly conjecture that Crabbe, by his satirical humour, had studied some peculiar local personality like Lord Huntingtower, better known about that time as Sir William Tollemache, or Talmash, who married, in 1790, Catherine, daughter of Francis Grey, Esq., from County Cork, and that it was her brother who represented the scapegoat of the family. They lived at Buckminster Park, a few miles beyond Grantham. Whether this brother-in-law is the Sir Eustace in the above-named poem will never be known. In any case, a few incidents there recorded are suggestive, where, especially, two dreadful demons are commanded to tempt him—one the Gambling Spirit, the other the Spirit of Mania. For example:

Alas ! they stay not for that call;
Spare me this woe ! ye demons, spare !—
They come ! the shrouded shadows, all—
'Tis more than mortal brain can bear;
Rustling they rise, they sternly glare
At man upheld by vital breath
Who led by wicked fiends should dare
To join the shadowy troops of death.
Yes, I have felt all man can feel,
Till he shall pay his nature's debt;
Ills that no hope has strength to heal,
No mind the comfort to forget:

> Whatever cares the heart can fret,
> The spirits wear, the temper gall,
> Woe, want, dread, anguish, all beset
> My sinful soul !—together all.

One particular friend just mentioned deserves our
attention for a moment, to introduce the story of " The
Dean's Lady " and his Cathedral. The son says that
soon after his father preached a visitation sermon at
Grantham in 1792, he " became intimately acquainted
with the late Dr. Gordon, . . . and my mother and
he passed some time with him at his residence near the
Cathedral."[1] And now, from a letter dated " Muston,
15 April, 1813," Crabbe writes: " Will you dine with
me on Sunday? I know among other good and
happy properties you can take the fare of the day as
it happens, and we can give you the Sunday joint and
apple-pye, in short, you shall have a country rector's
dinner, and now on this condition will you dine with
me?   Mrs. Crabbe and her sons desire their respectful
remembrances."[2] We may conclude from these few
words that Mrs. Gordon would be equally well known,
hence the following reference:

> Next, to a Lady I must bid adieu
> Whom some in mirth or malice call a " Blue."
> There needs no more—when that same word is said,
> The men grow shy, respectful and afraid;
> Save the choice friends who in her colour dress
> And all her praise in words like hers express.

> Why call a lady blue?   It is because
> She reads, converses, studies for applause;
> And therefore all that she desires to know
> Is just as much as she can fairly show.
> The real knowledge we in secret hide,
> It is the counterfeit that makes our pride.

>   Yes, I sometimes found
> A seat among a circle so profound
> While she, with grateful hand, a table spread,
> The Dean assenting—but the Dean is dead;

[1] Appendix I.: Belvoir Castle MSS.   [2] Mackay collection.

And though her sentiments are still divine
She asks no more her auditors to dine.[1]

And then before the final good-bye to his friends in
Lincoln:

In his Cathedral's gloom I pass'd my time,
Much in devotion, much in thought sublime:
There oft I paced the aisles and watched the glow
Of the sun setting on the stones below,
And saw the failing light that strove to pass
Through the dim coating of the storied glass,
Nor fell within, but till the day was gone
The red faint fire upon the window shone.
Then had I grief's proud thoughts, and said in tone
Of exultation, " World, I am alone !"
And saying this, I at the altar knelt,
And painful joys and rapturous anguish felt:
Till strong bold hopes possess'd me.

[1] " Posthumous Tales."

CHAPTER XXII

> Heaven would not all this woe for man intend
> If man's existence with his woe should end;
> Heaven would not pain and grief and anguish give,
> If man was not by discipline to live;
> And for that brighter, better world prepare,
> That souls with souls, when purified, shall share,
> Those stains all done away that must not enter there.[1]

APART from the happy nights at home, at Grantham, and in Lincoln, parochial troubles and family cares pressed heavily upon the parson's soul. Pluralism, though legal, had already left its ugly mark behind, for as a result of frequent changes (no less than eight curates-in-charge succeeding each other during the interregnum) and the spread of Methodism, the villagers built themselves a rival house, which is thought to have greatly diminished his flock. Someone rather singularly said:

> Wherever God erects a House of Prayer,
> The Devil always builds a Chapel there;
> And 'twill be found upon examination
> The latter has the largest congregation.

But then, owing to a split from the splitters, the statistics became questionable. At least, this is how the rector states the case:

> A sect remains, which though divided long
> In hostile parties, both are fierce and strong,
> And into each enlists a warm and zealous throng,
> Soon as they rose in fame, the strife arose,

---

[1] " Tales of the Hall."

168

TROWBRIDGE CHURCH.

TROWBRIDGE RECTORY.

facing p. 169.

The Calvinistic these, th' Arminian those;
With Wesley some remain'd, the remnant Whitfield chose.
Now various leaders both the parties take,
And the divided hosts their new divisions make.[1]

Then the constant indisposition of Myra, who suffered both physically and mentally, almost brought his life to an end. When she passed away, according to the tablet upon the north wall in the chancel, on September 21st, 1813, exhausted by anxiety and sleepless nights, the sorrowing husband collapsed. In the following May he went for a short visit to Aldeburgh, and gave one day to a solitary ramble among scenes so well remembered long ago, and wrote:

> Yes, I behold again the place,
> The seat of joy, the source of pain;
> It brings in view the form and face
> That I must never see again.
> The night-bird's song that sweetly floats
> On this soft gloom—this balmy air—
> Brings to the mind her sweeter notes
> That I again must never hear.
> Lo! yonder shines that window's light,
> My guide, my token, heretofore;
> And now again it shines as bright,
> When those dear eyes can shine no more.
> Then hurry from this place away!
> It gives not now the bliss it gave;
> For Death has made its charm his prey,
> And joy is buried in her grave.

On returning to Muston, where every scene still recalled painful remembrances and, as he said, " life was as tedious as a twice-told tale," his patron's successor presented him with the livings of Trowbridge and Croxton Kerrial.[2] Crabbe's induction to the Church and Rectory at Trowbridge, in Wiltshire,

---

[1] " The Borough."
[2] Appendix I.: Belvoir Castle MSS.

took place on June 3rd, 1814, by manorial right exercised through the marriage of Lady Frances Seymour, daughter of Charles, Duke of Somerset, with John, Marquis of Granby. The change from Leicestershire was a marked one in many respects. Here in the country, among rustics, sick and sorrowful, he fell into a rapid decline. Again, in his own words, he tells us: " I am now a solitary with a social dis-position, a hermit without a hermit's resignation." " What wonder," says his son, " that he was healthfully excited by the warm reception now experienced amongst the most cultivated families of the town and its vicinity." It always seemed to be the poet's opinion that at that crisis his system had, by a violent effort, thrown off some weight or obstruction which had been for many years previously giving his bodily condition the appear-ance of a gradual decline, afflicting him with occasional fits of low fever, and vexatiously disordering his digestive organs. Soon afterwards, however, he im-proved wonderfully. " His countenance," we are told, " was never ordinary, but health itself gives a new charm to any features, and his figure, which formerly had been rather thin and weakly, had now widened and rounded into a well-looking and dignified man."

George and John having been ordained, the former stayed behind to officiate at Croxton for some short time; the latter accompanied his father, and became curate of the parish. His devotion to duty soon allowed the Rector to leave him in charge whilst he journeyed up to London, where he made the acquaintance of other famous poets like Wordsworth, Southey, Rogers, Moore, and Campbell. He would often go to Bath to see and be seen by that fashionable community, and once went so far as Edinburgh in response to an urgent invitation from Sir Walter Scott during the Prince Regent's visit to Scotland. Mr. Gwynne, in his recent biography, tells a good story about this meeting. It was at a pageant. Scott, by right of his grandmother, appeared in a chief highland clan tartan, wearing trews, not kilts, when he noticed " the poet for whose works he had the greatest reverence and affection." " The first encounter of the bards was delightful, but Sir Walter had to attend his Majesty, on behalf of the city, and requested the gift of the glass from which he had drunk his health. He then deposited it in the safest pocket. Returning later to the poet, Scott neglected to guard his coat-tail, and sat down beside Crabbe. There was a crash, a scream, and a gesture of despair, and Scott had reason to be thankful that he wore the trews."

The refining influence gained by this wider experience can be slightly perceived in his last great effort, published during 1819, founded upon much family tattle and recollections of Aldeburgh and other places. Indeed, these " Tales of the Hall," as they are called, afford much more pleasure to read than the other lengthy compositions. They also have the distinguishing feature of forming rather a novel plan, happily devised by the author, in piecing them together. Indeed, so ingenious has he been in the process that many might be called the imaginary conversations between two brothers. Perhaps this belated discovery did, indeed, supply the needful tone lacking hitherto. Certainly, at last the most critical could hardly be dissatisfied on that score. For it is questionable whether anyone has produced quite the same effect in English verse, especially with such commonplace persons and themes. Take, for instance, that romantic and rustic story so simply styled "William Bailey."[1] Crabbe undoubtedly had been familiar with some incidents there recorded either at Belvoir or Allington, but it meant no slight stretch upon the imagination for him to harmonise the true with the fanciful. Even Southey said: " I was not disappointed with Crabbe's Tales. He is a decided mannerist, but so are all

[1] See Appendix II.

original writers in all ages; nor is it possible for a poet to avoid it, if he writes much in the same key and upon the same class of subjects."

Again, they are worth passing note here in helping us to sum up the clerical side of the poet's life. For " The Rector of the Parish " is Crabbe at Trowbridge, where he is seen facing a charge from scoffers and unbelievers.

> " A moral teacher !" some contemptuous cried.
> He smiled, but nothing of the fact denied,
> Nay, though he loved the minds of men to lead
> To the great points that form the Christian's creed,
> Still he offended, for he would discuss
> Points that to him seem'd requisite for us,
> Nor was this moral minister afraid
> To ask of inspiration's self the aid
> Of truths by him so sturdily maintain'd,
> That some confusion in the parish reign'd.
>   . . . Yet they all agreed,
> Whatever error had defiled his creed,
> His life was pure, and him they could commend,
> Not as their guide, indeed, but as their friend.

Indeed, one who knew him well observed: " He did not enjoy the happiness which many pastors express in being able to benefit their flocks; never was satisfied that he used the best means; and complained that men more imbued with a sense of the terrors of the Lord and less with His mercies succeeded better." Thus he has been considered Catholic and not Protestant at heart. Moreover, he lived, as a parson, far in advance of the times, for we are told how " particularly pleased and amused he used to be when conversing with the celebrated Beau Brummell "; that he took delight in going to the theatre occasionally; and had an admiration for Charles Kemble, to say nothing about racecourses which he also visited. Still, religion cannot be served by halves, and as another friend said, " He was more successful as a pastor than as a preacher," because " to his proper ministerial duties he ever attached great importance. He would put off a meditated journey rather than leave a poor parishioner who required his services, and from his knowledge of human nature he was able in a remarkable manner to throw himself into the circumstances of those who needed his help." And often in this respect his generous disposition became imposed upon, especially in his old age. Lastly, the biographer adds: " A benevolent gentle heart was seen in his manner and countenance, and no occasional hastiness of temper could conceal it—and then it soon became known that no one left his house unrelieved. But, above all, the liberality of his conduct with respect to Dissenters brought a counter-current in his favour. Though he was warmly attached to the established Church, he held that

> A man's opinion was his own, his due,
> And just possession, whether false or true.

And in all his intercourse with his much-divided parishioners he acted upon this principle." In the course of a few years, therefore, not only all opposition died away, but he became generally and cordially esteemed. They who differed from him admitted that he had a right also to his own religious opinions. And with regard to these he belonged more to the school of George Herbert than Jonathan Swift.

His diary and much correspondence[1] pertaining to this period are often both interesting and valuable. Here it is stated that on July 9th, 1825, when over seventy, he had the honour of being chosen a Justice of the Peace; and that after travelling and visiting " he always returned cheerfully to his duties, his charities, his poetry, and his fossils." So there we leave him, beloved by the family, and respected by all who knew him, till just before the end. Then some may like

[1] See Appendix I.—Examples and facsimile of a letter.

to share his priestly meditations, especially in connection with Scriptural doctrine so well expressed in such hymns as "The Resurrection," and another bearing upon the last "rites and ceremonies" of our Mother Church, "The Sacrament":

> O ! sacred gift of God to man,
>   A faith that looks above,
> And sees the deep, amazing plan
>   Of sanctifying love.
>
> Thou dear and yet tremendous God,
>   Whose glory pride reviles,
> How didst Thou change Thy awful rod
>   To pardoning grace and smiles ?
>
> Shut up with sin, with shame, below,
>   I trust this bondage past,
> A great, a glorious change to know,
>   And to be bless'd at last.
>
> I know Thou didst ordain for me,
>   Thy creature, bread and wine;
> The depth of grace I cannot see,
>   But worship the design.
>
> .　　　.　　　.　　　.
>
> 'Tis but a sleep—and Sion's King
>   Will call the many dead:
> 'Tis but a sleep—and then we sing
>   O'er dreams of sorrow fled.
>
> Yes !—wintry winds have ceased to blow,
>   And trembling leaves appear,
> And nature has her types to show
>   Throughout the varying year.

The Rev. George Crabbe died on February 3rd, 1832, in the seventy-eighth year of his age.

"Nature's sternest painter, yet her best."

APPENDIX I

BELVOIR CASTLE MANUSCRIPTS, ETC.

MUSTON,
GRANTHAM.
23rd Feb., 1814.

SIR,

His Grace the Duke of Rutland having expressed his intention of favouring me with the Presentations to the Rectory of Trowbridge in Wiltshire and to the Vicarage of Croxton Kerrial in this County (Leicestershire), I am directed to apply to . . . you to find those presentations for the Duke to sign . . . and I shall be further indebted to you if you will expedite the business so far as it may be done without inconvenience to you. My degree (one of Lambeth) is LL.B. and as Croxton is under value a dispensation I conclude is not wanted.

I am, Sir,
Your very obedient Servant,
GEORGE CRABBE.

I am at present Rector of Muston in this County and of West Allington in the County of Lincoln, and if any further information be necessary I must entreat that you will have the goodness to inform me : Muston, Grantham. Any papers or parcel with this direction will reach me without delay.

THOS. HILL MORTIMER, ESQ. *Solicitor,*
  ALBANY,
  PICCADILLY, LONDON.

LINCOLN.
Feb. 26, 1814.

SIR,

When I had the honour of addressing you from
Muston it did not occur to me that it might be necessary
to give you the information which I had (though not
from the first Authority) before received, viz. that
Trowbridge was lapsed to the Bishop of the Diocese,
yet as his Grace without adverting to this circumstance
desired the presentation both for that Rectory and the
Vicarage of Croxton to be laid before him for his
signature, I scarcely know whether I be correct in my
opinion that it become right for me to trouble you with
another letter, having consulted the Dean at whose
house I am on a visit, I learn no more than this, that
lapsed Livings are presented either by the Patron or
the Bishop, as the latter may or may not recede from
this claim, because though he may adopt the Patron's
views with respect to the Incumbent he may nevertheless choose to present to the Benefice himself.   All this
I am unwilling to omit, though it is very unlikely that
you should need any information or suggestions from
me: I will however in that case depend upon your
excusing my superfluous care.

I am, Sir,
Your very obedient Servant,
GEORGE CRABBE.

Croxton Kerrial being unattended by any doubts,
perhaps you will order the presentation to that Living
separately, as I shall be under the necessity of applying
to the Bishop of Lincoln for Institution to it in the first
instance.   Yet I should be glad if it be possible to have
one journey suffice for both Benefices.   I hope to have
the pleasure of receiving your letter at Muston whither
I expect to return on Monday or Tuesday the 28th
or 29th inst.   (*Ibid.*)

Sir

I was favored with your letter some time
since, and should have replied to you soon after, but I
heard that you were ill & thought it not worth of
sufficient Consequence to trouble you with. There was
also the word Vladies in the Receipt you sent for me
to sign, or which I meant to have made some alteration
but that is now rendered useless by some Conversation
which I had with a Gentleman at Belvoir Castle.
In all other Respect I make the acknowledgement
required I inclose it.

There was the same kind of Cred. between

it never has been adjusted & then written to him for last Bill — any & believe there is money due to me & shall direct that if you please to be paid to you & then whatever may be wanted I will make up on the next Rent day or when a few days after / that is, for the ½ 22. 6. 6 now due from me with the half years Rent added —

Mr Knighton was called to pay for the title deed, but I referred him to you as you had given me credit for it.

Buxton
March 6. 1813 — I am Sir

I am sorry that I neglected Your Your obedient Servant
Very Your humble Geo Gretton
but I got cover
Pray [?] his statement of Acct. which is now Jno Confederation

---

Facsimile of a letter in the author's possession—presented by the Rev. Canon D. W. Peregrine.

APPENDIX II

AN ALDEBURGH TRAGEDY

" THE BOAT RACE "

A Posthumous Tale, somewhat Abbreviated

I

The man who dwells where party-spirit reigns
May feel its triumphs, but must wear its chains;
He must the friends and foes of party take
For his, and suffer for his honour's sake;
When once enlisted upon either side,
He must the rude septennial storm abide—
A storm that, when its utmost rage is gone,
In cold and angry mutterings murmurs on:
A slow unbending scorn, a cold disdain,
Till years bring the full tempest back again.
Within our Borough two stiff sailors dwelt,
Who both this party storm and triumph felt;
Men who had talents, and were both design'd
For better things, but anger made them blind.
In the same year they married, and their wives
Had pass'd in friendship their yet peaceful lives,
And, as they married in a time of peace,
Had no suspicion that their love must cease.
In fact it did not; but they met by stealth,
And that perhaps might keep their love in health;
Like children watch'd, desirous yet afraid,
Their visits all were with discretion paid.
One Captain, so by courtesy we call
Our boy's commanders—they are captains all—
Had sons and daughters many; while but one
The rival Captain bless'd—a darling son.

Each was a burgess to his party tied,
And each was fix'd, but on a different side;
And he who sought his son's pure mind to fill
With wholesome food would evil too instil.
The last in part succeeded—but in part—
For Charles had sense, had virtue, had a heart;
And he had soon the cause of Nature tried
With the stern father, but this father died;
Who on his death-bed thus his son address'd:
" Swear to me, Charles, and let my spirit rest—
Swear to our party to be ever true,
And let me die in peace—I pray thee, do."

   With some reluctance, but obedience more,
The weeping youth reflected, sigh'd, and swore;
Trembling, he swore for ever to be true,
And wear no colour but the untainted Blue:
This done, the Captain died in so much joy,
As if he'd wrought salvation for his boy.

   The female friends their wishes yet retain'd,
But seldom met, by female fears restrain'd;
Yet in such town, where girls and boys must meet,
And every house is known in every street,
Charles had before, nay since his father's death,
Met, say by chance, the young Elizabeth;
Who was both good and graceful, and in truth
Was but too pleasing to th' observing youth;
And why I know not, but the youth to her
Seem'd just that being that she could prefer.
Both were disposed to think that party-strife
Destroy'd the happiest intercourse of life;
Charles, too, his growing passion could defend—
His father's foe he call'd his mother's friend.
Mothers, indeed, he knew were ever kind;
But in the Captain should he favour find?
He doubted this—yet could he that command
Which fathers love, and few its power withstand.

   The mothers both agreed their joint request
Should to the Captain jointly be address'd;

And first the lover should his heart assail,
And then the ladies, and if all should fail,
They'd singly watch the hour, and jointly might pre-
    vail.
   The Captain's heart, although unused to melt,
A strong impression from persuasion felt;
His pride was soften'd by the prayers he heard,
And then advantage in the match appear'd.
   At length he answer'd—" Let the lad enlist
In our good cause, and I no more resist;
For I have sworn, and to my oath am true,
To hate that colour, that rebellious Blue.
His father once, ere master of the brig,
For that advantage turn'd a rascal Whig:
Now let the son—a wife's a better thing—
A Tory turn, and say, God save the King !
For I am pledged to serve that sacred cause,
And love my country, while I keep her laws."
   The women trembled; for they knew full well
The fact they dare not to the Captain tell;
And the poor youth declared, with tears and sighs,
" My oath was pass'd; I dare not compromise."
   But Charles to reason made his strong appeal,
And to the heart—he bade him think and feel:
The Captain answering, with reply as strong—
" If you be right, then how can I be wrong ?
You to your father swore to take his part;
I to oppose it ever, head and heart;
You to a parent made your oath, and I
To God ! and can I to my Maker lie ?
Much, dear lad, I for your sake would do,
But I have sworn, and to my oath am true."
   Thus stood the parties when my fortunes bore
Me far away from this my native shore:
And who prevail'd, I know not—Young or Old;
But, I beseech you, let the tale be told.

II

POET: How fared these lovers? Many a time I
    thought
How with their ill-starr'd passion Time had wrought.
Did either party from his oath recede,
Or were they never from the bondage freed?
   FRIEND: Alas! replied my Friend—the tale I tell
With some reluctance, nor can do it well.
There are three females in the place, and they,
Like skilful painters, could the facts portray
In their strong colours—all that I can do
Is to present a weak imperfect view;
The colours I must leave—the outlines shall be true.
   Soon did each party see the other's mind,
What bound them both, and what was like to bind;
Oaths deeply taken in such time and place,
To break them now was dreadful—was disgrace!
  " That oath a dying father bade me take,
Can I—yourself a father—can I break?"
  " That oath which I a living sinner took,
Shall I make void, and yet for mercy look?"
   The women wept; the men, themselves distress'd,
The cruel rage of party zeal confess'd:
But solemn oaths, though sprung from party zeal,
Feel them we must, as Christians ought to feel.
   Yet shall a youth so good, a girl so fair,
From their obedience only draw despair?
Must they be parted? Is there not a way
For them both love and duty to obey?
Strongly they hoped; and by their friends around
A way, at least a lover's way, was found.
  " Give up your vote; you'll then no longer be
Free in one sense, but in the better free."
Such was of reasoning friends the kind advice,
And how could lovers in such case be nice?
A man may swear to walk directly on
While sight remains; but how if sight be gone?

" Oaths are not binding when the party's dead;
Or when the power to keep the oath is fled:
If I've no vote, I've neither friend nor foe,
Nor can be said on either side to go."
They were no casuists:—" Well !" the Captain cried,
" Give up your vote, man, and behold your bride !"
  Thus was it fix'd, and fix'd the day for both
To take the vow, and set aside the oath.
It gave some pain, but all agreed to say,
" You're now absolved, and have no other way:
'Tis not expected you should love resign
For man's commands, for love's are all divine."
  When all is quiet and the mind at rest,
All in the calm of innocence are blest;
But when some scruple mixes with our joy,
We love to give the anxious mind employ.
  In autumn late, when evening suns were bright,
The day was fix'd the lovers to unite;
But one before the eager Captain chose
To break, with jocund act, his girl's repose,
And, sailor-like, said, " Hear how I intend
One day, before the day of days, to spend !
All round the quay, and by the river's side,
Shall be a scene of glory for the bride.
We'll have a RACE, and colours will devise
For every boat, for every man a prize:
But that which first returns shall bear away
The proudest pendant—Let us name the day."
  They named the day, and never morn more bright
Rose on the river, nor so proud a sight;
Or if too calm appear'd the cloudless skies,
Experienced seamen said the wind would rise.
To that full quay from this then vacant place
Thronged a vast crowd to see the promised Race.
Mid boats new painted, all with streamers fair,
That flagg'd or flutter'd in that quiet air—
The Captain's boat that was so gay and trim,
That made his pride, and seem'd as proud of him—

Her, in her beauty, we might all discern,
Her rigging new, and painted on the stern,
As one who could not in the contest fail,
" Learn of *the little Nautilus* to sail."
　So forth they started at the signal gun,
And down the river had three leagues to run;
This sail'd, they then their watery way retrace,
And the first landed conquers in the race.
The crowd await till they no more discern,
Then parting say, " At evening we return."
　I could proceed, but you will guess the fate,
And but too well my tale anticipate.
　POET: True ! yet proceed.
　FRIEND: The lovers had some grief
In this day's parting, but the time was brief;
And the poor girl, between his smiles and sighs,
Ask'd, " Do you wish to gain so poor a prize ?"
　" But that your father wishes," he replied,
" I would the honour had been still denied:
It makes me gloomy, though I would be gay,
And oh ! it seems an everlasting day."
So thought the lass, and as she said farewell,
Soft sighs arose, and tears unbidden fell.
　The morn was calm, and ev'n till noon the strong
Unruffled flood moved quietly along;
In the dead calm the billows softly fell,
And mock'd the whistling sea-boy's favourite spell:
So rests at noon the reaper, but to rise
With mightier force and twofold energies.
The deep, broad stream moved softly, all was hush'd,
When o'er the flood the breeze awakening brush'd;
A sullen sound was heard along the deep,
The stormy spirit rousing from his sleep;
The porpoise rolling on the troubled wave,
Unwieldy tokens of his pleasure gave;
Dark, chilling clouds the troubled deep deform,
And led by terror downward rush'd the storm.
　As evening came, along the river's side,

Or on the quay, impatient crowds divide,
And then collect ; some whispering, as afraid
Of what they saw, and more of what they said,
And yet must speak: how sudden and how great
The danger seem'd, and what might be the fate
Of men so toss'd about in craft so small,
Lost in the dark, and subject to the squall.
Then sounds are so appalling in the night,
And, could we see, how terrible the sight;
None knew the evils that they all suspect,
And Hope at once they covet and reject.
   But where the wife, her friend, her daughter, where ?
Alas ! in grief, in terror, in despair—
At home, abroad, upon the quay.   No rest
In any place, but where they are not, best.
Fearful they ask, but dread the sad reply,
And many a sailor tells the friendly lie—
" There is no danger—that is, we believe,
And think—and hope "—but this does not deceive,
Although it soothes them, while they look around,
Trembling at every sight and every sound.
   Let me not dwell on terrors.—It is dark,
And lights are carried to and fro, and hark !
There is a cry—" A boat, a boat at hand !"
What a still terror is there now on land !
" Whose, whose ?" they all enquire, and none can
    understand.
   At length they come—and oh ! how then rejoice
A wife and children at that welcome voice:
It is not theirs—but what have these to tell ?
" Where did you leave the Captain—were they well ?"
Alas ! they know not, they had felt an awe
In dread of death, and knew not what they saw.
Thus they depart.—The evening darker grows,
The lights shake wildly, and as wildly blows
The stormy night-wind: fear possesses all,
The hardest hearts, in this sad interval.
   But hark again to voices loud and high !

Once more that hope, that dread, that agony,
That panting expectation ! " Oh ! reveal
What must be known, and think what pangs we feel !"
    In vain they ask ! The men now landed speak
Confused and quick, and to escape them seek.
Our female party on a sailor press,
But nothing learn that makes their terror less;
Nothing the man can show, or nothing will confess.
To some, indeed, they whisper, bringing news
For them alone, but others they refuse;
And steal away, as if they could not bear
The griefs they cause, and if they cause must share.
    They too are gone ! and our unhappy Three,
Half wild with fear, are trembling on the quay,
They can no ease, no peace, no quiet find,
The storm is gathering in the troubled mind;
Thoughts after thoughts in wild succession rise,
And all within is changing like the skies.
Their friends persuade them, " Do depart, we pray !"
They will not, must not, cannot go away,
But chill'd with icy fear, for certain tidings stay.
    And now again there must a boat be seen—
Men run together ! It must something mean !
Some figure moves upon the oozy bound
Where flows the tide. Oh ! what can he have found—
What lost ? And who is he ?—The only one
Of the loved three—the Captain's younger son.
Their boat was fill'd and sank. He knows no more,
But that he only hardly reach'd the shore.
He saw them swimming—for he once was near—
But he was sinking, and he could not hear:
And then the waves curl'd round him, but at length
He struck upon the boat with dying strength,
And that preserved him; when he turn'd around,
Nought but the dark, wild, billowy flood was found.
That flood was all he saw, that flood's the only sound—
Save that the angry wind, with ceaseless roar,
Dash'd the wild waves upon the rocky shore.

The Widows dwell together—so we call
The younger woman; widow'd are they all:
But she, the poor Elizabeth, it seems
Not life in her—she lives not, but she dreams;
She looks on Philip, and in him can find
Not much to mark in body or in mind—
He who was saved; and then her very soul
Is in that scene !—her thoughts beyond control,
Fix'd on that night, and bearing her along,
Amid the waters terrible and strong;
Till there she sees within the troubled waves
The bodies sinking in their wat'ry graves,
When from her lover, yielding up his breath,
There comes a voice—" Farewell, Elizabeth !"
    Yet Resignation in the house is seen,
Subdued Affliction, Piety serene,
And Hope for ever striving to instil
The balm for grief—" It is the Heavenly will:"
And in that will our duty bids us rest,
For all that Heaven ordains is good, is best;
We sin and suffer—this alone we know,
Grief is our portion, is our part below;
But we shall rise, that world of bliss to see,
Where sin and suffering never more shall be.

APPENDIX III

A BELVOIR ROMANCE

SELECTED FROM
" TALES OF THE HALL "—WILLIAM BAILEY
(*Abridged*)

A Visit to William and his Wife—His Dwelling—Story of
William and Fanny—Character of Both—Their Con-
tract—Fanny's Visit to an Aunt—Its Consequences—
Her Father's Expectation—His Death—William a
Wanderer—His Mode of Living—The Acquaintance
he forms—Travels across the Kingdom—Whom he
finds—The Event of their Meeting.

" I know," said George, " a happy man and kind,
Who finds his wife is all he wish'd to find,
A mild, good man, who, if he nothing sees,
Will suffer nothing to disturb his ease;
Who, ever yielding both to smiles and sighs,
Admits no story that a wife denies,—
She guides his mind, and she directs his eyes.
" Richard, there dwells within a mile a pair
Of good examples,—I will guide you there:
Such man is William Bailey,—but his spouse
Is virtue's self since she had made her vows:
I speak of ancient stories, long worn out,
That honest William would not talk about;
But he will sometimes check her starting tear,
And call her self-correction too severe.
" In their own inn the gentle pair are placed,
Where you behold the marks of William's taste:
They dwell in plenty, in respect, and peace,
Landlord and lady of the Golden Fleece:

Public indeed their calling—but there come
No brawl, no revel to that decent room;
All there is still, and comely to behold,
Mild as the fleece, and pleasant as the gold;
But mild and pleasant as they now appear,
They first experienced many a troubled year;
And that, if known, might not command our praise,
Like the smooth tenor of their present days.

" Our hostess, now so grave and steady grown,
Has had some awkward trials of her own:
She was not always so resign'd and meek,—
Yet can I little of her failings speak;
Those she herself will her misfortunes deem,
And slides discreetly from the dubious theme;
But you shall hear the tale that I will tell,
When we have seen the mansion where they dwell."
They saw the mansion—and the couple made
Obeisance due, and not without parade;
It was their duty—they were very sure
It was their pleasure.
     This they could endure,
Nor turn'd impatient. In the room around
Were care and neatness: instruments were found
For sacred music, books with prints and notes
By learned men and good, whom William quotes.
Next they beheld his garden, fruitful, nice,
And, as he said, his little paradise.
In man and wife appear'd some signs of pride,
Which they perceived not, or they would not hide.
This past, the visit was with kindness closed,
And George was ask'd to do as he proposed.

" Richard," said he, " though I myself explore
With no distaste the annals of the poor,
And may with safety to a brother show
What of my humble friends I chance to know,
Richard, there are who call the subjects low.

" The host and hostess of the Fleece—'tis base—
Would I could cast some glory round the place !

" The lively heroine once adorn'd a farm—
And William's virtue has a kind of charm:
Nor shall we, in our apprehension, need
Riches or rank—I think I may proceed:
Virtue and worth there are who will not see
In humble dress, but low they cannot be."

.   .   .   .   .

"The youth's addresses pleased his favourite maid,—
They wish'd for union, but were both afraid;
They saw the wedded poor,—and fear the bliss delay'd
Yet they appear'd a happier lass and swain
Than those who will not reason or refrain.

"William was honest, simple, gentle, kind,
Laborious, studious, and to thrift inclined;
More neat than youthful peasant in his dress,
And yet so careful, that it cost him less:
He kept from inns, though doom'd an inn to keep,
And all his pleasures and pursuits were cheap:
Yet would the youth perform a generous deed,
When reason saw or pity felt the need;
He of his labour and his skill would lend,
Nay, of his money, to a suffering friend.

"William had manual arts—his room was graced
With carving quaint, that spoke the master's taste;
But if that taste admitted some dispute,
He charm'd the nymphs with flageolet and flute.

"Constant at church, and there a little proud,
He sang with boldness, and he read aloud;
Self-taught to write, he his example took
And form'd his letters from a printed book.

"I've heard of ladies who profess'd to see
In a man's writing what his mind must be;
Our talents, tendencies, and likings trace,
And find for all the measure and the place:

"Strange times! when thus we are completely read
By man or woman, by the hand or head!
Believe who can,—but William's even mind
All who beheld might in his writing find;

His not the scratches where we try in vain
Meaning and words to construe or explain.
　" But with our village hero to proceed,—
He read as learned clerks are wont to read;
Solemn he was in tone, and slow in pace,
By nature gifted both with strength and grace.
　" Black parted locks his polish'd forehead press'd,
His placid looks an easy mind confess'd;
His smile content, and seldom more, convey'd;
Not like the smile of fair illusive maid,
When what she feels is hid, and what she wills betray'd.
　" The lighter damsels call'd his manner prim,
And laugh'd at virtue so array'd in him;
But they were wanton, as he well replied,
And hoped their own would not be strongly tried:
Yet he was full of glee, and had his strokes
Of rustic wit, his repartees and jokes;
Nor was averse, ere yet he pledged his love,
To stray with damsels in the shady grove;
When he would tell them, as they walk'd along,
How the birds sang, and imitate their song:
In fact, our rustic had his proper taste,
Was with peculiar arts and manners graced.
　" Frances, like William, felt her heart incline
To neat attire—but Frances would be fine:
Though small the farm, the farmer's daughter knew
Her rank in life, and she would have it too:
This, and this only, gave the lover pain.
He thought it needless, and he judged it vain:
Advice in hints he to the fault applied,
And talk'd of sin, of vanity, and pride.
　" ' And what is proud,' said Frances, ' but to stand
Singing at church, and sawing thus your hand ?
Looking at heaven above, as if to bring
The holy angels down to hear you sing ?
And when you write, you try with all your skill,
And cry, no wonder that you wrote so ill !
For you were ever to yourself a rule,

And humble add, you never were at school—
Is that not proud ?—And I have heard beside,
The proudest creatures have the humblest pride:
If you had read the volumes I have hired,
You'd see your fault, nor try to be admired;
For they who read such books can always tell
The fault within, and read the mind as well.'

" William had heard of hiring books before,
He knew she read, and he inquired no more;
On him the subject was completely lost,
What he regarded was the time and cost;
Yet that was trifling—just a present whim,
' Novels and stories !   What were they to him ?'

" With such slight quarrels, or with those as slight,
They lived in love, and dream'd of its delight.
Her duties Fanny knew, both great and small,
And she with diligence observed them all;
If e'er she fail'd a duty to fulfil,
'Twas childish error, not rebellious will;
For her much reading, though it touch'd her heart,
Could neither vice nor indolence impart.

.   .   .   .   .

" Yet, when from William and her friends retired,
She found her reading had her mind inspired
With hopes and thoughts of high mysterious things,
Such as the early dream of kindness brings;
And then she wept, and wonder'd as she read,
And new emotions in her heart were bred:
She sometimes fancied that when love was true
'Twas more than she and William ever knew;
More than the shady lane in summer-eve,
More than the sighing when he took his leave;
More than his preference when the lads advance
And choose their partners for the evening dance;
Nay, more than midnight thoughts and morning dreams
Or talk when love and marriage are the themes;
In fact, a something not to be defined,

Of all subduing, all commanding kind,
That fills the fondest heart, that rules the proudest mind.
  " But on her lover Fanny still relied,
Her best companion, her sincerest guide,
On whom she could rely, in whom she would confide.
  " All jealous fits were past; in either now
Were tender wishes for the binding vow;
There was no secret one alone possess'd,
There was no hope that warm'd a single breast;
Both felt the same concerns their thoughts employ,
And neither knew one solitary joy.
  " Then why so easy, William ? why consent
To wait so long ? thou wilt at last repent;
' Within a month,' does Care and Prudence say,
If all be ready, linger not a day;
Ere yet the choice be made, on choice debate,
But having chosen, dally not with fate.

   .   .   .   .   .

  " While yet to wait the pair were half content,
And half disposed their purpose to repent,
A spinster-aunt, in some great baron's place,
Would see a damsel, pride of all her race:
And Fanny, flatter'd by the matron's call,
Obey'd her aunt, and long'd to see the Hall;
For halls and castles in her fancy wrought,
And she accounts of love and wonder sought;
There she expected strange events to learn,
And take in tender secrets fond concern;
There she expected lovely nymphs to view,
Perhaps to hear and meet their lovers too;
The Julias, tender souls ! the Henrys kind and true:
There she expected plottings to detect,
And—but I know not what she might expect—
All she was taught in books to be her guide,
And all that nature taught the nymph beside.
  " Now that good dame had in the castle dwelt
So long that she for all its people felt;

She kept her sundry keys, and ruled o'er all,
Female and male, domestics in the hall;
By her lord trusted, worthy of her trust,
Proud but obedient, bountiful but just.
    " She praised her lucky stars, that in her place
She never found neglect, nor felt disgrace;
To do her duty was her soul's delight,
This her inferiors would to theirs excite,
This her superiors notice and requite;
To either class she gave the praises due,
And still more grateful as more favour'd grew:
Her lord and lady were of peerless worth,
In power unmatch'd, in glory and in birth;
And such the virtue of the noble race,
It reach'd the meanest servant in the place;
All, from the chief attendant on my lord
To the groom's helper, had her civil word;
From Miss Montregor, who the ladies taught,
To the rude lad who in the garden wrought;
From the first favourite to the meanest drudge,
Were no such women, heaven should be her judge;
Whatever stains were theirs, let them reside
In that pure place, and they were mundified;
The sun of favour on their vileness shone,
And all their faults like morning mists were gone.
    " There was Lord Robert ! could she have her choice,
From the world's masters he should have her voice;
So kind and gracious in his noble ways,
It was a pleasure speaking in his praise:
And Lady Catherine—O ! a prince's pride
Might by one smile of hers be gratified;
With her would monarchs all their glory share,
And in her presence banish all their care.
    " Such was the matron, and to her the maid
Was by her lover carefully convey'd.
    " When William first the invitation read
It some displeasure in his spirit bred,
Not that one jealous thought the man possess'd,

He was by fondness, not by fear distress'd;
But when his Fanny to his mind convey'd
The growing treasures of the ancient maid,
The thirty years, come June, of service past,
Her lasting love, her life that would not last;
Her power ! her place ! what interest ! what respect
She had acquired—and shall we her neglect ?

   " ' No, Frances, no !' he answered, ' you are right;
But things appear in such a different light !'

   " Her parents blest her, and as well became
Their love advised her, that they might not blame:
They said, ' If she should earl or countess meet
She should be humble, cautious, and discreet;
Humble, but not abased, remembering all
Are kindred sinners—children of the fall;
That from the earth our being we receive,
And are all equal when the earth we leave.'

   " They then advised her in a modest way
To make replies to what my lord might say;
Her aunt would aid her, who was now become
With nobles noble, and with lords at home.

          .   .   .   .   .

So went the pair; and William told at night
Of a reception gracious and polite;
He spake of galleries long and pictures tall,
The handsome parlours, the prodigious hall;
The busts, the statues, and the floors of stone,
The storied arras, and the vast saloon,
In which was placed an Indian chest and screen,
With figures such as he had never seen:
He told of these as men enraptured tell,
And gave to all their praise, and all was well.

   " Left by the lover, the desponding maid
Was of the matron's ridicule afraid;
But when she heard a welcome frank and kind,
The wonted firmness repossess'd her mind;
Pleased by the looks of love her aunt display'd,
Her fond professions, and her kind parade.

14

" In her own room, and with her niece apart,
She gave up all the secrets of her heart;
And, grown familiar, bid her Fanny come,
Partake her cheer, and make herself at home.

" Shut in that room, upon its cheerful board
She laid the comforts of no vulgar hoard;
Then press'd the damsel both with love and pride,
For both she felt—and would not be denied.

" Grace she pronounced before and after meat,
And bless'd her God that she could talk and eat;
Then with new glee she sang her patron's praise—
' He had no paltry arts, no pimping ways;
She had the roast and boil'd of every day,
That sent the poor with grateful hearts away;
And she was grateful—Come, my darling, think
Of them you love best, and let us drink.'

" And now she drank the healths of those above,
Her noble friends, whom she must ever love;
But not together, not the young and old,
But one by one, the number duly told;
And told their merits too—there was not one
Who had not said a gracious thing or done;
Nor could she praise alone, but she would take
A cheerful glass for every favourite's sake,
And all were favourites—till the rosy cheek
Spoke for the tongue that nearly ceased to speak;
That rosy cheek that now began to shine,
And show the progress of the rosy wine;
But there she ended—felt the singing head,
Then pray'd as custom will'd, and so to bed.

" The morn was pleasant, and the ancient maid
With her fair niece about the mansion stray'd;
There was no room without th' appropriate tale
Of blood and murder, female sprite or male;
There was no picture that th' historic dame
Pass'd by and gave not its peculiar fame;
The births, the visits, weddings, burials, all
That chanced for ages at the noble Hall.

" These and each revolution she could state,
And give strange anecdotes of love and hate;
This was her first delight, her pride, her boast,
She told of many an heiress, many a toast,
Of Lady Ellen's flight, of Lord Orlando's ghost;
The maid turn'd pale, and what should then ensue
But wine and cake—the dame was frighten'd too.

" The aunt and niece now walk'd about the grounds,
And sometimes met the gentry in their rounds;
' Do let us turn !' the timid girl exclaim'd.
' Turn !' said the aunt, ' of what are you ashamed ?
What is there frightful in such looks as those ?
What is it, child, you fancy or suppose ?
Look at Lord Robert, see if you can trace
More than true honour in that handsome face !

" ' What ! you must think, by blushing in that way,
My lord has something about love to say,
But I assure you that he never spoke
Such things to me in earnest or in joke,
And yet I meet him in all sorts of times,
When wicked men are thinking of their crimes.

" ' There ! let them pass.—Why, yes, indeed 'tis true
That was a look, and was design'd for you;
But what the wonder when the sight is new ?
For my lord's virtue you may take my word,
He would not do a thing that was absurd.'

" A month had pass'd; ' And when will Fanny come ?'
The lover ask'd, and found the parents dumb;
They had not heard for more than half the space,
And the poor maiden was in much disgrace;
Silence so long they could not understand,
And this of one who wrote so neat a hand.
Their sister sure would send were aught amiss,
But youth is thoughtless—there is hope in this.

" As time elapsed, their wonder changed to wo,
William would lose another day, and go;
Yet if she should be wilful and remain,
He had no power to take her home again;

But he would go.—He went, and he return'd,—
And in his look the pair his tale discern'd;
Stupid in grief, it seem'd not that he knew
How he came home, or what he should pursue:
Fanny was gone !—her aunt was sick in bed,
Dying, she said—none cared if she were dead;
Her charge, his darling, was decoy'd, was fled !
But at what time, and whither, and with whom,
None seem'd to know—all surly, shy, or dumb.
　" Each blamed himself, all blamed the erring maid,
They vow'd revenge; they cursed their fate, and pray'd.

. . . . .

Moved by his grief, the father sought the place,
Ask'd for his girl, and talk'd of her disgrace;
Spoke of the villain, on whose cursed head
He pray'd that vengeance might be amply shed;
Then sought his sister, and beheld her grief,
Her pain, her danger,—this was no relief.
　" ' Where is my daughter ? bring her to my sight !'—
' Brother, I'm rack'd and tortured day and night.'—
' Talk not to me !　What grief have you to tell,
Is your soul rack'd, or is your bosom hell ?
Where is my daughter ?'—' She would take her oath
For their right doing, for she knew them both,
And my young lord was honour.'—' Woman, cease !
And give your guilty conscience no such peace—
You've sold the wretched girl, you have betray'd your
　　niece.'—
' The Lord be good ! and O ! the pains that come
In limb and body—brother, get you home !
Your voice runs through me,—every angry word,
If he should hear it, would offend my lord.'
　" ' Has he a daughter ? let her run away
With a poor dog, and hear what he will say !
No matter what, I'll ask him for his son.'—
' And so offend ?　Now, brother, pray be gone !'
　" My lord appear'd, perhaps by pity moved,
And kindly said he no such things approved;

Nay, he was angry with the foolish boy,
Who might his pleasures at his ease enjoy;
The thing was wrong—he hoped the farm did well,—
The angry father doom'd the farm to hell;
He then desired to see the villain-son,
Though my lord warn'd him such excess to shun;
Told him he pardon'd, though he blamed such rage,
And bade him think upon his state and age.
   " ' Think ! yes, my lord ! but thinking drives me mad.
Give me my child !—Where is she to be had ?
I'm old and poor, but I with both can feel,
And so shall he that could a daughter steal !
Think you, my lord, I can be so bereft
And feel no vengeance for the villian's theft ?
Old if I am, could I the robber meet
I'd lay his breathless body at my feet—
Was that a smile, my lord ? think you your boy
Will both the father and the child destroy ?'
   " My lord replied—' I'm sorry from my soul !
But boys are boys, and there is no control.'
   " ' So, for your great ones Justice slumbers then !
If men are poor they must not feel as men—
Will your son marry ?'—' Marry !' said my lord,
' Your daughter ?—marry—no, upon my word !'
   " ' What then, our stations differ !—but your son
Thought not of that—his crime has made them one,
In guilt united—she shall be his wife,
Or I th' avenger that will take his life !'
   " ' Old man, I pity and forgive you; rest
In hope and comfort—be not so distress'd,
Things that seem bad oft happen for the best;
The girl has done no more than thousands do,
Nor has the boy—they laugh at me and you.'—
' And this my vengeance—curse him !'—' Nay, forbear;
I spare your frenzy, in compassion spare.'
   " ' Spare me, my lord ! and what have I to dread ?
O ! spare not, heaven, the thunder o'er his head—
The bolt he merits !'

                              Such was his redress;
And he return'd to brood upon distress.

    .   .   .   .

  " And what of William ?—William from the time
Appear'd partaker both of grief and crime;
He cared for nothing, nothing he pursued,
But walk'd about in melancholy mood;
He ceased to labour—all he loved before
He now neglected, and would see no more;
He said his flute brought only to his mind
When he was happy, and his Fanny kind;
And his loved walks, and every object near,
And every evening-sound she loved to hear,
The shady lane, broad heath, and starry sky,
Brought home reflections, and he wish'd to die:
Yet there he stray'd, because he wish'd to shun
The world he hated, where his part was done;
As if, though lingering on the earth, he there
Had neither hope nor calling, tie nor care.
  " At length a letter from the daughter came,
' Frances ' subscribed, and that the only name;
She ' pitied much her parents, spoke of fate,
And begg'd them to forget her, not to hate;
Said she had with her all the world could give,
And only pray'd that they in peace should live,—
That which is done, is that we're born to do,
This she was taught, and she believed it true;
True, that she lived in pleasure and delight,
But often dream'd and saw the farm by night;
The boarded room that she had kept so neat,
And all her roses in the window-seat;
The pear-tree shade, the jasmine's lovely gloom,
With its long twigs that blossom'd in the room;
But she was happy, and the tears that fell
As she was writing had no grief to tell;
We weep when we are glad, we sigh when we are well.'
  " A bill inclosed, that they beheld with pain
And indignation, they return'd again;

There was no mention made of William's name,
Check'd as she was by pity, love, and shame.
  " William, who wrought for bread, and never sought
More than the day demanded when he wrought,
Was to a sister call'd, of all his race
The last, and dying in a distant place;
In tender terror he approached her bed,
Beheld her sick, and buried her when dead:
He was her heir, and what she left was more
Than he required, who was content before.
With their minds' sufferings, age, and growing pain,
That ancient couple could not long remain,
Nor long remain'd; and in their dying groan
The suffering youth perceived himself alone;
For of his health or sickness, peace or care,
He knew not one in all the world to share;
Now every scene would sad reflections give,
And most his home, and there he could not live;
There every walk would now distressing prove,
And of his loss remind him, and his love.

.   .   .   .   .

  " With the small portion by his sister left
He roved about as one of peace bereft,
And by the body's movements hoped to find
A kind of wearied stillness in the mind,
And sooner bring it to a sleepy state,
As rocking infants will their pains abate.
  " Thus careless, lost, unheeding where he went,
Nine weary years the wandering lover spent.

.   .   .   .   .

  " His sole employment, all that could amuse,
Was his companions on the road to choose;
With such he travell'd through the passing day,
Friends of the hour, and walkers by the way;
And from the sick, the poor, the halt, the blind,
He learn'd the sorrows of his suffering kind.

" He learn'd of many how unjust their fate,
For their connexions dwelt in better state;
They had relations famous, great or rich,
Learned or wise, they never scrupled which;
But while they cursed these kindred churls, would try
To build their fame, and for their glory lie.

" Others delighted in misfortunes strange,
The sports of fortune in her love for change.

" Some spoke of wonders they before had seen,
When on their travels they had wandering been;
How they had sail'd the world about, and found
The sailing plain, although the world was round;
How they beheld for months th' unsetting sun;
What deeds they saw ! what they themselves had done !

" But female vagrants would at times express
A new-born pleasure at the mild address;
His modest wish, clothed in accent meek,
That they would comfort in religion seek.

" And some would freely on his thoughts intrude,
And thrust themselves 'twixt him and solitude:
They would his faith and of its strength demand,
And all his soul's prime motions understand:
How ! they would say, such woe and such belief,
Such trust in heaven, and yet on earth such grief !
There is the strong man yet that keeps his own,
Who by a stronger must be overthrown;
There is the burden that must yet be gone,
And then the pilgrim may go singing on.
He felt the comfort, and began to pray
For such companions on the king's highway.

 . . . .

" William had now across the kingdom sped,
To th' eastern ocean from St. David's Head;
And wandering late, with various thoughts oppress'd,
'Twas midnight ere he reach'd his place of rest,—
A village inn, that one way-faring friend
Could from experience safely recommend,

Where the kind hostess would be more intent
On what he needed than on what he spent;
Her husband, once a heathen, she subdued,
And with religious fear his mind imbued;
Though his conviction came too late to save
An erring creature from an early grave.

" Since that event, the cheerful widow grew
In size and substance,—her the brethren knew,—
And many friends were hers, and lovers not a few;
But either love no more could warm her heart,
Or no man came who could the warmth impart.

" William drew near, and saw the comely look
Of the good lady, bending o'er her book;
Hymns it appear'd,—for now a pleasing sound
Seem'd as a welcome in his wanderings found:
He enter'd softly, not as they who think
That they may act the ruffian if they drink,
And who conceive, that for their paltry pence
They may with rules of decency dispense;
Far unlike these was William,—he was kind,
Exacting nothing, and to all resign'd.

.   .   .   .   .

" He saw the hostess reading,—and their eyes
Met in good will, and something like surprise:
It was not beauty William saw, but more,
Something like that which he had loved before—
Something that brought his Fanny to his view,
In the dear time when she was good and true;
And his, it seem'd, were features that were seen
With some emotion—she was not serene:
And both were moved to ask what looks like those could
        mean.
At first she colour'd to the deepest red,
That hurried off, till all the rose was fled;
She call'd a servant, whom she sent to rest,
Then made excuse to her attentive guest;
She own'd the thoughts confused,—'twas very true,
He brought a dear departed friend in view:

Then, as he listen'd, bade him welcome there
With livelier looks and more engaging air,
And stirr'd the fire of ling, and brush'd the wicker chair,
Waiting his order with the cheerful look,
That proved how pleasant were the pains she took.
  " He was refresh'd.   They spake on various themes—
Our early pleasures, Reason's first-drawn schemes,
Youth's strong illusions, Love's delirious dreams:
Then from her book he would presume to ask
A song of praise, and she perform'd the task:
The clock struck twelve.   He started—' Must I go ?'
His looks spoke plainly, and the lady's, ' No:'
So down he sat,—and when the clock struck one
There was no start, no effort to be gone:
Nor stay'd discourse—
        ' And so your loves were cross'd,
And the loved object to your wishes lost ?
But was she faithless, or were you to blame ?
I wish I knew her—will you tell her name ?
Excuse me—that would hurt her if alive;
And, if no more, why should her fault survive ?
But love you still ?'—
        ' Alas ! I feel I do,
When I behold her very looks in you !'
  " ' Yet, if the frail one's name must not be known,
My friendly guest may trust me with his own.'
  " This done, the lady paused, and then replied—
' It grieves me much to see your spirit tried;—
But she was like me,—how I came to know
The lamb that stray'd I will hereafter show;—
We were indeed as sisters.   Should I state
Her quiet end, you would no longer hate:
I see your heart,—and I shall quickly prove,
Though she deserved not, yet she prized your love:
Long as she breathed was heard her William's name—
And such affection half absolves her shame.
  " ' Weep not, but hear me, how I came to know
Thee and thy Frances—this to heaven I owe !

And thou shalt view the pledge, the very ring,
The birth-day token—well you know the thing;
" This," if I ever—thus I was to speak,
As she had spoken—but I see you weak:
She was not worthy——'
                        ' O! you cannot tell
By what accursed means my Fanny fell !
What bane, compulsion, threats—for she was pure;
But from such toils what being is secure ?
Force, not persuasion, robb'd me——'
                        ' You are right;
So has she told me, in her Maker's sight:
She loved not vice——'
                        ' O ! no—her heart approved
All that her God commanded to be loved;
And she is gone——'
                        ' Consider ! death alone
Could for the errors of her life atone.'
    " ' Speak not of them; I would she knew how dear
I hold her yet !—But dost thou give the tear
To my loved Frances ?—No ! I cannot part
With one who has her face, who has her heart;
With looks so pleasing, when I thee behold,
She lives—that bosom is no longer cold—
Then tell me—art thou not—in pity speak—
One whom I sought, while living meant to seek ?—
Art thou my Fanny ?—Let me not offend—
Be something to me—be a sufferer's friend—
Be more—be all !—The precious truth confess—
Art thou not Frances ?'
                        ' O, my William ! yes !
But spare me, spare thyself, and suffer less:
In my best days, the spring-time of my life,
I was not worthy to be William's wife;
A widow now—not poor, indeed—not cast
In outer darkness—sorrowing for the past,
And for the future hoping—but no more:
Let me the pledges of thy love restore,

And give the ring thou gavest—let it be
A token still of my regard for thee,—
But only that,—and to a worthier now
Consign the gift.'

            ' The only worthy thou !'
Replied the lover; and what more express'd
May be omitted—here our tale shall rest.

.   .   .   .   .

  " This pair, our host and hostess of the Fleece,
Command some wealth, and smile at its increase;
Saving and civil, cautious and discreet,
All sects and parties in their mansion meet;
There from their chapels teachers go to share
The creature-comforts,—mockery grins not there;
There meet the wardens at their annual feast,
With annual pun—' the parish must be fleeced;'
There traders find a parlour cleanly swept
For their reception, and in order kept;
And there the sons of labour, poor but free,
Sit and enjoy their hour of liberty.
  " So live the pair,—and life's disasters seem
In their unruffled calm a troubled dream;
In comfort runs the remnant of their life—
He the fond husband, she the faithful wife."

Facsimile of a letter in the author's possession—presented by the Rev. Canon D. W. Peregrine.

INDEX

PRINTED IN GREAT BRITAIN BY
BILLING AND SONS LTD., GUILDFORD AND ESHER